Lily Cooper

Guardian of Light
Protection and Healing with Archangel Michael

Copyright © 2024 L. A. Santos
All rights reserved.
No part of this book may be reproduced in any form or by any means without written permission from the copyright holder.
Cover image © L. A. Santos Studio
Review by Marco Avelar
Graphic design by Tania Navarro
Layout by Paulo Xavier
All rights reserved to:
L. A. Santos
Category: Spirituality

Summary

Prologue 5
Chapter 1 Awakening to the Presence of Archangel Michael 8
Chapter 2 Strengthening Your Spiritual Connection 13
Chapter 3 Preparing for Rituals with Michael 18
Chapter 4 Invoking Michael's Assistance 23
Chapter 5 Understanding the Sacred Symbols 28
Chapter 6 Working with the Sword of Light 33
Chapter 7 Activating the Shield of Protection 38
Chapter 8 Balancing with the Divine Scale 43
Chapter 9 Transmuting with the Blue Flame 48
Chapter 10 Integrating Michael's Attributes 53
Chapter 11 Angelic Initiation Ritual 59
Chapter 12 Meditating with Michael's Presence 64
Chapter 13 Receiving Divine Guidance 69
Chapter 14 Building Your Energetic Self-Defense 74
Chapter 15 Emotional Healing with Michael's Support 79
Chapter 16 Restoring Physical Health 84
Chapter 17 Purifying Environments with Michael 89
Chapter 18 Daily Spiritual Protection 94
Chapter 19 Overcoming Fears with Michael's Help 99
Chapter 20 Freeing Yourself from Harmful Habits 104
Chapter 21 Manifesting Goals with Michael 109
Chapter 22 Cultivating Inner Peace 114
Chapter 23 Connecting with the Angelic Hierarchy 119
Chapter 24 Ritual of Consecration to Michael 124

Chapter 25 Enhancing Your Angelic Communication 129
Chapter 26 Aligning with the Divine Purpose 134
Chapter 27 Astral Travels with Michael's Protection............... 139
Chapter 28 Facilitating Group Healings 144
Chapter 29 Recognizing Michael as Messenger 149
Chapter 30 Dedicating Yourself to a Spiritual Mission............ 154
Chapter 31 Attaining Spiritual Ascension 159
Chapter 32 Celebrating Sacred Festivities 164
Chapter 33 Exploring Esoteric Teachings 169
Chapter 34 Honoring the Spiritual Legacy 174
Chapter 35 Miracles and Divine Interventions 179
Chapter 36 Aligning with Cosmic Cycles................................... 184
Chapter 37 Manifesting Abundance with Michael 189
Chapter 38 Finding Support in Transitions.............................. 194
Chapter 39 Expanding Your Multidimensional Perception...... 199
Chapter 40 Collaborating with Elemental Angels 204
Chapter 41 Michael as Patron of Warriors................................ 209
Chapter 42 Extending the Connection to Family...................... 214
Chapter 43 Applying the Teachings in Daily Life..................... 219
Epilogue 224

Prologue

There is a moment when you feel a silent call, a gentle whisper that touches your heart and defies the world around you. A presence that transcends the ordinary and evokes a dimension that, although invisible, manifests for those ready to perceive it. This book, which you now hold in your hands, is a portal that connects you to that dimension, a space where the physical and spiritual intertwine, where the protection and strength of an eternal guardian, Archangel Michael, await those who open themselves to his light.

Since time immemorial, Michael has been humanity's defender, a presence echoing through the ages and crossing cultures and beliefs. But he is not merely a figure of ancient legends; he is real, tangible to those who sincerely seek him. He is the one who offers his sword of light to cut through illusions and his shields to protect the essence of who you truly are. With Michael by your side, you not only find courage but discover that this courage has always existed within you, waiting to be awakened.

Now, let each page of this book be a bridge, a path that draws you closer to this connection. This book is not just a read; it is a living guide, a link to a force that illuminates and protects. Michael is present in the words, in the energy flowing from each chapter, in each symbol and practice described here. As you progress through this reading, you will not just read—you will feel his presence—a strong and constant energy, an unconditional support for every moment of doubt, challenge, or vulnerability.

Perhaps you have already sensed this inexplicable force at some moment, a breath of confidence amidst fear, a feeling of peace during times of anguish. It could have been a small coincidence, an unexpected feather, a ray of light in a dark moment, or a sudden intuition bringing you clarity. These are signs from the archangel, small invitations for you to recognize his presence. And in that recognition, you open a path to a transformative relationship.

The journey with Michael is not passive, nor immediate. It demands that you surrender to the unknown, that you cultivate a daily space for connection, allowing Michael's light to penetrate and illuminate every aspect of your life. As you read this book, you will enter a new dynamic of self-awareness and surrender, where challenges become opportunities for growth, where doubt dissolves into confidence, and where shadows yield to the power of light. With Michael, protection is more than defense; it is an awakening to your own potential.

This is not a book about Michael. It is a path to knowing him, an experience that places you directly under his protective mantle, enveloping you in an invisible armor of peace and clarity. The teachings here will guide you in practices and rituals that amplify your connection with him, allowing you to feel his presence in your daily life, in moments of tranquility and turmoil. Each symbol, each flame, each invoked word is a key that opens the portal to his strength and support.

As you walk through these pages, you will be activating Archangel Michael's power in your life. You will feel the energy of his sword, cutting through the bonds of old fears and limiting beliefs, creating new space for what truly matters. His shield will envelop you like a sphere of light, protecting you from influences that no longer serve your greater good, allowing your own light to shine unobstructed. And as you deepen this connection, you will realize that Michael not only protects you but awakens a strength within you, a dormant potential that simply needed to be acknowledged.

This book is for you, for the awakening of the warrior who lives within. It is a call for you to discover yourself as strong and protected, guided by a force that will never abandon you. Michael is beside you now, ready to extend his protection and power into your life. With each page, you will walk closer to this presence, closer to a light that transforms, protects, and guides. Move forward; allow yourself to know this sacred presence, for the journey you are about to embark on is more than a reading. It is the beginning of a new reality, where you and Michael walk together, and where you will find the true security and power that have always resided within you.

Chapter 1
Awakening to the Presence of Archangel Michael

In the quiet moments of dawn and dusk, in those pauses where time seems suspended, there lies an opportunity for communion with a force beyond sight—a radiant figure who has watched over humanity since the earliest ages. Archangel Michael, known throughout cultures and faiths as the warrior of light, the defender, the messenger, beckons those who seek protection, guidance, and strength. His presence is both gentle and powerful, often felt as a subtle shift in energy or sensed through signs that resonate deep within the soul. Awakening to Michael's presence is not only about noticing his influence but opening oneself fully to a realm where the material and spiritual intertwine, a place where boundaries dissolve and understanding blooms.

To recognize Archangel Michael in your life is to tune into an ancient symphony, one that calls to the courageous and the devoted. For as long as humans have sought protection from unseen dangers, Michael has been the celestial sentinel, bearing the sword of divine truth and justice. But to sense him requires not just intention, but a softening of the heart and a sharpening of the inner senses. His presence often starts as an impression—an almost magnetic pull that leaves one feeling supported and safeguarded. He manifests through light, often in hues of blue or gold, and brings an energy of clarity and fortitude that fills even the most vulnerable spaces within us.

This journey begins with awareness, for awareness opens the portal to Michael's realm. For many, the first glimpse comes in moments of despair or difficulty when an unexplainable surge of courage or peace arises from within, as though Michael himself stands beside them. In other instances, his influence can be noticed in recurring symbols or words that subtly appear throughout the day—a vivid dream, a feather found at your doorstep, or the sudden gleam of light at the corner of one's vision. These may seem like coincidences, but they are Michael's way of reaching out, calling us to acknowledge his enduring guardianship.

Attuning to his presence requires more than recognizing signs; it demands an attunement of one's inner frequency, a quieting of the mind, and a clearing of the heart. Michael's domain exists within the vibrational planes of courage, strength, and love. To reach him, one must cultivate these qualities within, as though polishing a mirror to catch the light. The ritual of awakening begins by creating sacred moments each day to sit in silence, allowing the mind to drift into a state of surrender. This is not a passive emptiness but a readiness to receive—a willingness to listen to the voice that does not speak in words.

Start each morning by invoking a prayer or intention, one that opens your spirit to Michael's light. Let it be simple, perhaps something like, "Archangel Michael, guardian of light, reveal your presence in my life. Let me walk in strength, protected and guided by your wisdom." Even as these words are spoken, imagine a vast blue light enveloping you, a light that is alive, pulsating with warmth and purpose. You may find that as you recite this intention, a wave of calm envelops you, a gentle but unmistakable reminder that you are not alone.

But words alone are only part of the journey. Visualizing Michael, picturing his image with a sword of truth and a shield of light, helps anchor his energy in your mind and heart. See him as a being of immense strength and compassion, standing by your side, his wings sweeping outward, ready to shield you from any harm. Imagine his sword, not as a weapon of war, but as a beacon that cuts through illusions and fears. Feel his strength infuse your own heart, filling you with a confidence that transcends personal limitations.

Pay attention to the sensations that arise during these moments. Michael's energy can be felt as a surge of warmth in the chest, a tingling on the skin, or a sudden clarity of mind. He comes with an unmistakable force, a vibrational signature that feels both uplifting and grounding. While his presence can inspire awe, it is also marked by a profound gentleness that offers peace and reassurance. Over time, these experiences become clearer, more distinct. With each mindful breath, you are creating a bridge to his realm, a pathway that grows stronger with use, like footsteps forming a trail through the woods.

As you build this connection, the signs of Michael's presence will begin to manifest with greater frequency and in more tangible ways. He communicates through synchronicities, symbols, and a heightened intuition that often feels like a whisper guiding you in the right direction. For instance, the sudden appearance of the name "Michael" in unexpected places, whether in conversation or a book title, may be an indication of his attention upon you. Feathers, particularly blue or white, may also be among his calling cards, left as subtle reminders that you are under his protection. In dreams, he may appear as a figure of light or a warrior standing against shadows, offering guidance through symbols and imagery that speaks to your innermost needs and desires.

The journey to recognize Michael's presence is as unique as each soul that embarks upon it. Some may feel an immediate connection, while others may experience his influence slowly, like a seed taking root in the soil. For those who seek a deeper bond, it may be helpful to dedicate a small altar or sacred space to Michael in your home. Place a blue candle, a symbol of his heavenly light, and perhaps a small statue or image of him as a focal point for your prayers and meditations. Each time you pass by, offer a silent prayer or touch your heart in gratitude, acknowledging his presence in your life.

Nature, too, can be a powerful ally in connecting with Michael. The natural world resonates with his essence, from the resilience of mountains to the clarity of flowing waters. Spend time in places that evoke a sense of peace and strength, letting the energy of these sacred spaces remind you of his ever-watchful presence. If possible, stand under a vast sky, breathe deeply, and imagine Michael's light descending from the heavens, enveloping you in a cocoon of protection. Such moments, steeped in stillness and reverence, foster a receptivity that goes beyond the ordinary, allowing Michael's energy to flow into your heart without interference.

Once this connection is established, it becomes a part of your being. You may find that certain situations, which once caused you anxiety or fear, are now met with a newfound calm. This is Michael's gift, for his presence has a transformative effect that strengthens the heart and aligns the mind with a higher purpose. Through him, courage becomes more than an emotion—it becomes a state of existence, a lens through which the world is viewed and understood.

Embracing Archangel Michael's presence is an act of faith, a surrender to the unseen forces of good that tirelessly work for our welfare. It is to acknowledge that we walk alongside a protector who is ever-present, one who does not tire or falter, whose light is as eternal as the stars. And while he may appear as a figure of strength and authority, his deepest desire is to awaken those same qualities within us, to see us walk boldly on our paths with open hearts and steady minds.

As this awareness deepens, there will be moments when you feel an unshakable certainty that Michael is with you. Perhaps it will come as a vision of light, a sense of warmth in a moment of fear, or an undeniable sign that could only be his doing. Each time you sense him, remember that his presence is a reminder of your own divine potential. In seeking him, you are not only inviting a guardian but a guide, one who will walk beside you, empowering you to become a beacon of light, just as he is.

Through this quiet yet profound awakening, you come to realize that the boundary between you and the archangel is not as solid as it seems. His strength becomes your own, his courage flows through your veins, and his unwavering dedication to truth and justice awakens a divine purpose within you. Embrace this journey with openness, and let each moment of connection serve as a bridge to realms beyond sight, to a world where Archangel Michael's light shines brightly, forever illuminating your path.

Chapter 2
Strengthening Your Spiritual Connection

To walk a path with Archangel Michael is to commit not only to his protection but to an evolving, deepening spiritual relationship. Like any connection of profound value, it requires intention, dedication, and the nurturing of a receptive heart. Strengthening this bond is a practice, a discipline that grows over time and reveals new layers of wisdom and support with each step. This is the way of communion with Michael—a journey both humbling and transformative.

Those who seek Michael's companionship often feel a calling, an inner urge to connect with his energy beyond mere invocation. The resonance of his essence invites us to explore realms of the spirit where courage, clarity, and divine truth dwell. To strengthen your connection with him is to cultivate the qualities he embodies, creating within yourself a sanctuary where his presence can naturally flow. Michael's light is like a river; to receive it fully, you must first prepare a place within where it can be held and nurtured.

Begin this journey by setting a sacred intention. Intentions act as the invisible hand that guides us, a beacon that sends our soul's desires outward, aligning us with spiritual forces beyond our conscious understanding. Choose an intention that resonates deeply with you, one that expresses your genuine desire to connect with Archangel Michael. It might be a simple phrase, such as, "I open my heart to Michael's guidance and protection" or "I walk in the courage and strength of Archangel Michael."

Repeat it daily, allowing its words to settle deeply in your spirit, letting each repetition strengthen the bond you are building.

With this intention as your foundation, create rituals that bring you closer to his presence. These rituals do not have to be elaborate; they simply need to be consistent, a regular gesture that signals your commitment to this sacred connection. One practice to consider is lighting a candle each morning or evening—a blue or white candle, if possible, as these colors are often associated with Michael. As you light it, visualize the flame as a portal to his world, a bridge that allows his light to fill your space and your heart. As the candle burns, imagine it dispelling any shadows around you, symbolizing the clarity and courage that Michael brings.

Quieting the mind and preparing the heart are essential steps in this process, for Michael's presence is not always loud or obvious. His energy flows quietly, subtly, like the morning light that illuminates the sky gradually, until everything is bathed in radiance. Meditation is a powerful tool for tuning into this subtler realm. Begin by sitting in silence, closing your eyes, and focusing on your breath. With each inhalation, visualize drawing in Michael's light, allowing it to fill every part of you. As you exhale, release any doubts or fears that may cloud your ability to connect. Let this rhythm of breath bring you into a space of inner stillness, a sanctuary where Michael's energy can be received without interference.

Over time, this meditative practice will open your awareness, sharpening your ability to perceive the shifts in energy that signal his presence. Michael's energy is distinct: a combination of strength and peace that feels simultaneously grounding and uplifting. As you meditate, imagine his presence as a pillar of blue light standing beside or behind you, an unyielding force of protection and love. Feel this light envelop you, forming an impenetrable shield around your aura, a barrier that keeps out negative energies and thoughts. Let this visualization become as real as possible, letting your imagination become the doorway to a genuine experience.

Another way to strengthen your bond is through the practice of journaling. Dedicate a notebook to your spiritual experiences with Michael, a place where you can record the thoughts, signs, dreams, or feelings that arise as you walk this path. Writing down your intentions, observations, and reflections anchors your experiences, making them tangible and real. You may find that as you write, insights and messages from Michael begin to flow naturally. He often communicates through subtle impressions or shifts in emotion, which can easily go unnoticed if not captured in writing. Reflecting on these entries over time allows you to see the progression of your relationship, the ways in which his presence and guidance shape your journey.

Nature is another ally in fostering this spiritual connection. Michael's essence is intertwined with the forces of nature, and time spent outdoors can amplify his presence. Visit a place that brings you peace, perhaps a forest, a mountain, or near the waters of a lake or ocean. Feel the solid ground beneath your feet, the stability and resilience of the earth, and allow these elements to remind you of Michael's strength. The natural world carries a purity that aligns well with his energy, making it easier to feel his guidance and protection. Spend time in these places not only to connect with him but to cleanse your spirit, allowing the rhythms of nature to balance and ground you.

Symbols and objects can also be used as conduits for Michael's energy, enhancing your connection in daily life. Consider wearing or carrying a small symbol associated with him, such as a pendant shaped like a sword or shield, or a crystal like blue sapphire, lapis lazuli, or angelite, all stones traditionally connected to Michael's energy. These symbols serve as reminders, subtle points of focus that help you keep his energy close, even in the midst of daily routines. When you hold these objects or touch them, let them act as anchors, grounding you in his strength and protection.

Dreamwork offers yet another avenue for deepening your bond. Michael often appears to seekers through dreams, using this quiet space of the subconscious to impart messages or to bring a sense of peace and protection. Before you go to bed, set the intention to receive guidance from him, asking that any messages be revealed to you clearly and in a way you will understand. Place a small object that represents him—like a blue stone or feather—by your bedside, a silent invitation for him to enter your dream space. Keep your journal nearby to capture any symbols, impressions, or messages upon waking, as these insights often fade quickly. Over time, these dreams may begin to form a mosaic, small pieces of wisdom that connect to reveal a larger picture of his guidance in your life.

Perhaps most importantly, stay attuned to the everyday moments that hint at his presence. Michael is not bound to the ethereal; he walks alongside those who call upon him, influencing the tangible world. You may notice that during challenging times, an unexplainable strength arises within you, or a person appears just when you need support. These are moments where Michael's influence is subtle but profound, an unseen hand guiding and protecting. Pay attention to these instances; they are the footprints of his presence in your life, markers of a relationship that goes beyond ritual or intention, grounded instead in a genuine communion of spirit.

Strengthening this connection is not a destination but a lifelong journey. Michael's presence, once awakened, becomes a source of enduring support, an energy you can rely on even when the world feels uncertain or overwhelming. And as this connection matures, it begins to shape you from within, transforming fears into courage, uncertainty into clarity. In Michael's light, you find not only a protector but an example of steadfast devotion, an inspiration to walk your path with unwavering faith.

At times, this bond may grow so strong that Michael's guidance feels like a part of you, an inner voice that speaks with clarity and conviction. When you face decisions or moments of doubt, you may hear his presence as a nudge towards truth, a gentle push away from anything that is not aligned with your highest self. This is the depth of connection that can be achieved, a communion that transcends the boundaries of the physical world, entering into a sacred partnership where you become, in a sense, a reflection of his strength and purpose.

Know that this journey is unique to each soul. Some may feel Michael's presence as a quiet companion, always near but rarely seen, while others may experience his energy more dramatically. However he appears, remember that this connection is your own, shaped by your intentions, your experiences, and the depths of your heart. As you strengthen this bond, you are not just connecting to an archangel; you are aligning with a profound force of divine love and protection, one that has watched over countless souls through the ages.

In the silence, in the candle's flame, in the grounding presence of nature, and the symbols that carry his essence, Michael's energy can be felt, experienced, and known. Trust in this connection, nurture it with devotion, and allow it to guide you on a path illuminated by the courage and wisdom of Archangel Michael.

Chapter 3
Preparing for Rituals with Michael

In the ancient traditions, the call to invoke a divine presence required more than words or gestures—it demanded an alignment of body, mind, and spirit, a complete attunement to the sacred energy one sought to commune with. To prepare for rituals with Archangel Michael is to honor this practice of sacred preparation, to purify oneself in spirit and heart so that his power may flow without resistance. For Michael, the defender of truth and justice, requires a space free of doubts, distractions, and shadows. As we approach him with reverence, our preparation becomes a signal of readiness, a testament to our respect for his profound presence.

The journey of preparation begins in the inner sanctum, the space of one's heart and mind, where true intention resides. Preparing yourself to receive Michael's light is not only about cleansing the outer space but about turning inward to clear and harmonize your own energy. This act of cleansing is an offering in itself, a way of saying to Michael, "I come before you pure, ready, and devoted." It is in this inner stillness, this quiet and receptive state, that his presence can be most deeply felt.

Begin with a purification ritual, an act of clearing not only the physical space where you will call upon Michael but also the energetic field within yourself. There are several ways to approach this, each designed to cleanse both the seen and unseen layers of your being. First, consider the ancient practice of smudging. Using a bundle of sage or palo santo, light it and let the smoke cleanse your ritual space. Move slowly, wafting the smoke into every corner, paying special attention to places where energy might feel heavy or stagnant. As the smoke rises, visualize any negative or dense energies dissipating, leaving a space that is clear, calm, and ready to welcome Michael's divine light.

Next, consider the power of water as a cleansing force. Water, as a symbol of purity, is revered across cultures for its ability to wash away impurities and refresh the spirit. Before beginning the ritual, take a few moments to wash your hands or face with intention, allowing the water to cleanse not only physically but energetically. If possible, a full bath infused with purifying salts, like Epsom or sea salt, can help to release any lingering negativity or tension. Visualize the water drawing out and dissolving any worries, stress, or residual energy that may interfere with the ritual. Imagine that with each drop, you are being reborn, your spirit renewed and attuned to the sacred.

Beyond physical cleansing, the mind too must be prepared. A cluttered mind is like a fogged mirror; it distorts perception and blocks the clarity needed to connect deeply with Michael's presence. Meditation serves as an ideal practice for centering the mind and creating a state of inner peace. Sit in silence for a few moments, breathing slowly and evenly, letting each exhale release the tensions and distractions of daily life. Imagine your thoughts becoming quieter, like leaves settling upon still waters. Let this quietude bring you into the present, into a space where time feels suspended and your spirit feels grounded, ready to receive.

With your physical and mental energies aligned, the next step is to set your intention for the ritual. The power of intention cannot be understated—it is the seed from which all energy flows, the focus that gives purpose and direction to your work with Michael. As you prepare, ask yourself what it is you seek from his guidance: protection, strength, clarity, or perhaps wisdom on a particular matter. Allow this intention to crystallize in your heart, giving it form and clarity. Speak it aloud if you wish, letting your words serve as a beacon that calls out to Michael, signaling your readiness to connect with his divine energy.

Anointing is another powerful step in the preparation process, an act that creates a bridge between the physical and spiritual worlds. Certain essential oils, when used with reverence, can enhance your connection to Michael's energy. Frankincense, myrrh, and sandalwood are especially potent, known for their spiritual properties that uplift and purify. Place a drop of oil on your wrists or forehead, areas considered energetically receptive. As you do so, visualize Michael's light merging with your own, creating a shield that surrounds you and protects you as you open yourself to his guidance. Feel this shield as an embrace, a cocoon of his strength and love enveloping you, making you feel safe and empowered.

With each layer of preparation, you are building a vessel for Michael's presence—a sacred space within and around you that resonates with his essence. As the ritual space becomes imbued with purity and intention, the act of invocation becomes not only a call but a welcome, an invitation for Michael to step into a prepared and consecrated environment. Candles can be an essential part of this atmosphere, their flickering flames symbolizing the light that Michael brings into darkness. A blue or white candle, colors that correspond to his energy, may be placed at the center of your space. As you light it, say a silent prayer, dedicating this flame to his guidance and protection. Visualize it as a beacon that reaches beyond the physical realm, calling Michael to your side.

When everything is in place, take a moment to connect with the earth beneath you. Michael's power is one of grounding as much as it is of celestial strength, for he is the bridge between heaven and earth, grounding divine truth in the material world. Feel your feet firmly on the ground or imagine roots extending from your body, anchoring you deeply into the earth. This grounding practice stabilizes your energy, creating a balance that enables you to remain present, clear, and aligned as you work with Michael's energy. In this grounded state, you become a channel through which his energy can flow unimpeded, allowing the full force of his presence to come through.

With each preparation, each mindful step, you are not only opening a door to Michael's energy but showing respect to the sacredness of this encounter. In the stillness of your space, listen closely. You may begin to feel a shift, a gentle yet undeniable sensation that you are no longer alone. Michael's energy can manifest as a soft hum, a subtle warmth, or a vibration in the air around you. Honor this presence, for in that moment, you are in communion with a force that transcends earthly concerns, a power that guides, protects, and uplifts.

If you feel guided, consider using sacred words or invocations as you reach out to Michael. Language, when spoken with intention, becomes a conduit for divine energy. A simple invocation might be, "Archangel Michael, I call upon you now. May your light and protection surround me, may your strength and courage fill my heart." As you speak, let each word resonate within you, sending a pulse of energy outward. Feel the atmosphere shift as you speak, an affirmation that your words have been received, that Michael is present, attentive, and ready to guide.

Crystals can also serve as conduits for Michael's energy. Certain stones, particularly those in shades of blue or clear quartz, can be placed around your space or held in your hand as you prepare. Blue stones such as lapis lazuli, sodalite, or blue kyanite align well with Michael's energy, amplifying your intentions and helping to anchor his presence. Hold the stone in your hand, feeling its energy, and imagine it connecting you to Michael, a channel through which his protection and strength flow into your being. After the ritual, keep this stone close to you as a reminder of his ongoing presence in your life.

In this prepared and sanctified space, you are ready to begin your work with Michael. Whether you seek his protection, guidance, or healing, know that each ritual brings you closer to his presence, each prayer, and intention a step deeper into his light. The act of preparation is not merely a formality—it is a transformation, a shift from the ordinary to the sacred, an opening of the self to divine energy. As you stand at the threshold of this sacred space, Michael meets you not only as an archangel but as a guardian, a protector, and a friend.

Remember, too, that every ritual you perform with Michael is an act of devotion, a reaffirmation of your connection to his light. With each ritual, you weave a bond that grows stronger, an invisible thread that links your soul to his eternal strength. The deeper this bond becomes, the more naturally you will feel his presence, and the more powerfully his light will guide and protect you.

As you complete your ritual, take a moment to offer gratitude. Gratitude is the language of the heart, the soul's way of acknowledging the gifts it has received. In the silence, thank Michael for his presence, for the light and protection he brings, and for his enduring guidance. This gratitude forms the closing of your ritual, a final offering that seals the space with love and reverence. Know that each time you return to this space, each time you prepare yourself with this care and devotion, you deepen your connection to Michael's energy, creating a bridge that grows stronger with every step you take along this sacred path.

Chapter 4
Invoking Michael's Assistance

The act of invocation is an ancient art, a calling that bridges realms, inviting divine energies into our world. To invoke Archangel Michael is to summon not just protection, but a force of courage, clarity, and unwavering truth. Michael's presence offers guidance through trials, strength in the face of fear, and a light that penetrates even the densest shadows. Invoking his assistance, however, requires more than words; it is a communion, an alignment of the heart and spirit with the energies he embodies. In this invocation, you are inviting Michael into your life—not merely as a distant protector, but as a companion and ally on your path.

The essence of invoking Michael lies in intention. Intention shapes the energy you direct, guiding it with purpose and clarity. When calling upon Michael, your intention should be clear and pure, free from fear or doubt. It is this clarity of purpose that calls Michael's attention, for his energy aligns naturally with strength, truth, and love. Before you begin, center yourself in stillness, grounding your mind and emotions. Feel your connection to the earth, the stability it provides, and let this grounding serve as an anchor for the energy you are about to call forth.

A powerful way to prepare for this invocation is by focusing on your breath. Breathing is not only a source of physical life but an entryway to the spirit. Begin by taking deep, deliberate breaths, inhaling through the nose and exhaling slowly through the mouth. With each breath, release any tension or lingering thoughts, allowing your mind to enter a state of quiet openness. Imagine each inhalation drawing Michael's light into your being, filling you with his courage and strength. Each exhalation releases doubts or fears, clearing space within you for his presence.

Visualize yourself surrounded by light—a radiant, protective sphere that separates you from the distractions and chaos of the outer world. This sphere is your sacred space, a place of safety and peace where only energies aligned with love and truth may enter. Imagine this light expanding, growing brighter and stronger with each breath, forming a beacon that calls to Michael. This is your signal to him, a light in the vast expanse that draws his presence nearer, guiding him to you.

When you feel centered and ready, speak the invocation aloud. Michael's presence responds powerfully to the spoken word, for words carry the vibration of your heart's intent. You may create your own words or use a traditional invocation, such as: "Archangel Michael, guardian and protector, I call upon you now. Surround me with your light, grant me your strength, and guide me with your wisdom. I invite your presence here; may I feel your courage and be shielded by your power." Let each word resonate in the space around you, imagine your voice as a bridge to his realm, reaching through dimensions to where he dwells.

As you speak, visualize Michael's presence taking form before you. Imagine him standing tall, a powerful figure bathed in a light of celestial blue. See the gleam of his armor, his sword of light in hand, a symbol of truth and justice. His wings stretch wide, encompassing you in a circle of protection. Feel his gaze upon you, a presence that is both compassionate and strong. Let this vision become vivid, allowing every detail to fill your mind. As you do so, open your heart to receive his energy, allowing it to flow into you as a steady stream of light, grounding you in strength and filling you with a profound sense of peace.

The sensations that follow may vary. Michael's presence is often felt as warmth, a tingling sensation, or an undeniable calm. His energy may stir emotions, bringing up feelings you may not have expected. Know that whatever arises is part of his work, a clearing and strengthening of your spirit. Remain open to these sensations, trusting in his wisdom. If emotions surface, allow them to flow without judgment, letting Michael's light cleanse and transform them into strength and clarity.

To deepen the connection, visualize Michael's sword. This sword is not just a weapon; it is a symbol of divine truth, a tool to cut through illusions and falsehoods. Imagine him holding it before you, its blade shining with pure light. If you seek guidance or clarity on a particular issue, now is the time to ask. Formulate your question clearly in your mind or speak it aloud, directing it toward Michael with trust and openness. You may sense a response through words that enter your mind, a shift in energy, or a feeling of certainty that emerges within you. Michael's answers often come as subtle impressions, whispers of truth that align deeply with your intuition.

For those seeking protection, envision Michael's shield surrounding you. His shield is a barrier of pure light, an energetic wall that blocks all harm and negativity. As you visualize it, feel it forming around you like an impenetrable fortress, a sanctuary that nothing can breach. This shield becomes a part of your energetic field, not only during the invocation but as a lasting protection that accompanies you. With Michael's shield, you walk through the world in confidence, knowing that you are guarded by an archangel whose presence is unyielding and constant.

If you wish to carry Michael's protection with you beyond this moment, consider creating a symbol or physical reminder. A small crystal, such as a piece of blue kyanite, angelite, or clear quartz, can hold the energy of his presence. Hold the crystal in your hand as you invoke him, asking that it be charged with his protection. As you do this, imagine the crystal absorbing his light, becoming a reservoir of his energy that you can carry with you. Keep this crystal close—a talisman that holds the power of his protection, a reminder of his guardianship that you can turn to whenever you need strength.

The invocation may also be enhanced by the use of sacred symbols. Michael's sigil, a symbol associated with his energy, can serve as a powerful tool for focusing his presence. Draw this sigil on a small piece of paper, a candle, or even your skin. As you trace its lines, visualize it glowing with blue light, vibrating with his energy. The sigil acts as a conduit, a sign that you are calling upon him with reverence and devotion. In your heart, know that he recognizes this sign, that it is a language beyond words, one he responds to with immediate awareness.

As you complete the invocation, take a few moments to sit in silence, letting Michael's energy settle within and around you. This is a time of receiving, a moment to allow his presence to fully integrate with your own. You may feel a deep calm or a surge of courage, a sense of alignment with something vast and unshakable. Hold this feeling close, knowing that it is the imprint of Michael's spirit, a reminder of the bond you have just strengthened. In these moments, you are not merely asking for assistance; you are merging with his light, becoming a vessel for the courage, clarity, and protection he embodies.

To close the invocation, offer a word of gratitude. Gratitude grounds the energy and completes the circle of invocation, a gesture that shows respect and acknowledgment for the presence you have invited. Simply say, "Thank you, Archangel Michael, for your protection, for your guidance, and for your light." As you speak, visualize his form beginning to dissolve, the light around you gently dimming. Know that he does not leave you; his energy remains in your heart, a constant presence that you can call upon whenever you need. The closing of the invocation is not a goodbye but a transition, a release of the formal ritual that allows his influence to permeate your life naturally.

When you stand from this invocation, carry forward the sense of his energy, knowing that it is woven into the fabric of your being. Michael's presence remains with you, not as a fleeting visitation but as a lasting alliance, a partnership that grows stronger each time you invoke him. Trust in this bond, knowing that with each call, he comes closer, answering not only your words but the silent call of your heart.

In your daily life, remember that invoking Michael does not require elaborate rituals or words. Simply calling his name with genuine need and reverence is enough. As you walk this path, the line between invocation and presence begins to blur, until the invocation becomes unnecessary. Michael's energy will be there, as close as your own heartbeat, a guardian whose strength lives within you. His courage becomes your courage, his clarity your clarity. This is the gift of invocation—a transformation, a merging, a becoming.

By inviting Archangel Michael's assistance, you are not merely summoning a protector; you are calling upon a force that inspires your highest self, guiding you to live with truth and courage. In his presence, fear falls away, shadows retreat, and you walk forward, illuminated by his light. Through each invocation, you align more deeply with his energy, shaping a life that reflects his strength, wisdom, and compassion. With Michael beside you, the path ahead shines brightly, each step guided, each moment held in the light of his eternal guardianship.

Chapter 5
Understanding the Sacred Symbols

In the rich tapestry of spiritual practices, symbols hold a unique place. They are carriers of ancient power, each one a doorway to realms of meaning and mystery. Symbols associated with Archangel Michael are among the most potent, embodying qualities of protection, justice, and divine truth. To understand these sacred symbols is to connect with the very essence of Michael's mission and presence. Each one carries a frequency, a pulse of energy that aligns with the virtues he embodies, and working with these symbols allows us to tune into his presence on a deeper, more resonant level.

The first and perhaps most recognized symbol associated with Archangel Michael is his **sword**. This is not a mere weapon of combat but a beacon of divine truth, a symbol of purity and clarity that pierces through illusions and shadows. Known as the "Sword of Light," it represents the power to cut away falsehoods, negativity, and any energetic ties that hinder growth. Michael's sword shines with a radiant blue flame, a color that carries the vibration of protection, courage, and divine will. When visualized or invoked, the sword becomes an extension of Michael's energy, a tool for spiritual warriors who seek to walk in truth.

To connect with the energy of Michael's sword, imagine it within your hand, glowing with intense, clear light. Picture it cutting through any cords of fear, doubt, or attachment that hold you back. This visualization can be done in meditation or as part of a ritual where you call upon Michael's assistance. By working with the symbol of the sword, you invite his energy to act as a guide, revealing what is true and removing obstacles that obscure your path. It's a powerful tool for those moments in life when clarity is needed, when discernment is essential, and when you are called to release old patterns that no longer serve your highest self.

The **shield** is another sacred symbol closely connected to Michael. Just as his sword represents truth and justice, his shield embodies the power of protection and safety. The shield is a barrier against harm, a boundary that guards against unwanted energies and negative influences. Michael's shield is often visualized as a circle of light or as an actual shield engraved with sacred symbols, shining with an aura of deep, unwavering strength. It represents not just defense but the strength to stand firm, grounded in the light of divine protection.

When invoking the shield, imagine it surrounding your entire being, a shimmering barrier that blocks all negativity from entering your space. See it deflecting any harmful thoughts, fears, or energies directed toward you, allowing only love and light to flow through. In moments of vulnerability or fear, visualizing Michael's shield around you creates a sense of security and calm, a reminder that you are never truly alone, that you walk with divine protection. Carrying a small talisman or wearing a piece of jewelry in the shape of a shield can serve as a constant reminder of Michael's watchful presence, a symbol you can touch to instantly reconnect with his energy.

Beyond the sword and shield, Michael's **scales** are another profound symbol. Known as the "Divine Scales," they represent balance, justice, and divine order. The scales reflect Michael's role as an arbiter of justice, a force that seeks equilibrium and harmony in all things. To work with the scales is to align oneself with fairness, to seek truth in all actions, and to weigh one's heart and intentions carefully. The scales are a reminder that each thought, word, and deed carries weight and that walking the path of truth requires a deep commitment to honesty, not only with others but with oneself.

When seeking balance in life, visualize Michael's scales. Imagine placing your concerns, desires, or dilemmas upon one side of the scales, and let Michael's light bring balance to them. This practice helps you see matters from a higher perspective, balancing emotional impulses with wisdom and clarity. As you work with this symbol, you may begin to notice a shift in your approach to life, an awareness of how each choice contributes to the balance of your inner and outer worlds. The scales teach patience, responsibility, and a commitment to living in harmony with the highest principles of fairness and truth.

The **blue flame** is another sacred symbol tied to Michael, embodying his energy in a pure, powerful form. The blue flame is a symbol of divine transformation, a fire that does not consume but purifies. It represents the burning away of negativity, the transmutation of lower energies into higher frequencies of love and truth. Michael's blue flame is often described as vibrant, intense, a flame that radiates a frequency that aligns with the throat chakra, the center of communication and expression. Working with this flame invites Michael's assistance in transforming fear into courage, anger into compassion, and confusion into clarity.

To invoke the blue flame, imagine it surrounding your body, cleansing and purifying your energy field. See it dissolving any dark or heavy energies, transforming them into light. Feel the warmth of this flame as a comforting presence, a reminder of Michael's unwavering support. This visualization can be particularly powerful during times of inner conflict, fear, or when faced with challenging situations. The blue flame acts as both a purifier and a protector, a force that clears the way for truth and love to flourish. It is a symbol of Michael's ability to transmute even the most difficult energies, a reminder that in his presence, all things can be transformed for the better.

Another powerful yet lesser-known symbol associated with Michael is the **halo of light**. This halo is often visualized as a crown of blue or golden light encircling the head. It signifies spiritual insight, divine wisdom, and the presence of higher guidance. The halo represents Michael's connection to the divine, his role as a channel for God's wisdom and will. Wearing or visualizing this halo invites higher perspectives, helping one see beyond personal fears and limitations into the broader truths of existence. It is a symbol of enlightenment, clarity, and a mind attuned to divine wisdom.

To work with the halo of light, close your eyes and imagine a ring of blue or gold light above your head. Feel its energy descending, filling your mind with clarity and aligning you with higher wisdom. This practice can be helpful in times of uncertainty or when making important decisions, allowing Michael's wisdom to guide your thoughts and actions. The halo brings a sense of peace and confidence, a reminder that you are connected to divine guidance, that your mind is in tune with the light of higher understanding.

Each of these symbols—the sword, shield, scales, blue flame, and halo—carry a distinct vibration and purpose, yet they are united by their connection to Michael's energy. Working with them is a form of devotion, a way of aligning oneself with the qualities that Michael represents. These symbols act as keys, unlocking different aspects of his guidance and protection. They can be used individually or together, depending on your needs and intentions. By incorporating these symbols into your spiritual practice, you create a direct link to Michael's energy, allowing his presence to manifest in your life in tangible ways.

Beyond visualization, you may choose to incorporate these symbols into physical objects, such as jewelry, altar items, or written sigils. Carving or drawing these symbols on candles, stones, or even small pieces of paper can turn these objects into powerful focal points for your rituals and prayers. When you meditate, hold these objects close, feeling their connection to Michael, letting them serve as conduits for his energy. These symbols are tools, ways to connect, to anchor, and to embody his qualities within yourself.

The language of symbols is the language of the soul, a communication that transcends words and reaches the deepest parts of our being. In working with Michael's symbols, you are learning this language, creating a dialogue with his energy that speaks to you through impressions, feelings, and insights. The symbols teach without speaking, guiding you to embody Michael's strength, wisdom, and protection in your daily life.

As you become more familiar with these symbols, you may find that they begin to appear in your dreams or in moments of intuition. Michael often communicates through symbols, using them as reminders or signs of his presence. A vision of a sword, a shield, or a blue flame in a dream can be his way of assuring you, of letting you know that he is with you, guiding and protecting you. Trust these signs, for they are messages from a realm beyond sight, a realm where Michael's presence is constant and unwavering.

In understanding these sacred symbols, you are not only learning about Michael but stepping into a deeper relationship with him. Each symbol is an invitation to embody the qualities it represents, a call to integrate Michael's energy into your life in practical, transformative ways. Through his sword, you find the courage to face truth; through his shield, the strength to stand firm; through his scales, the wisdom to seek balance; through his blue flame, the ability to transform; and through his halo, the clarity to perceive divine wisdom.

These symbols are more than images; they are living connections to Michael's essence, bridges that bring his light into our world. Embrace them, work with them, and let them guide you on your path. In doing so, you invite Michael to walk with you, to stand beside you, and to fill your life with the strength, protection, and guidance that his presence bestows.

Chapter 6
Working with the Sword of Light

The Sword of Light, wielded by Archangel Michael, is a symbol that transcends the physical realm. It is not merely a weapon but a sacred tool of divine truth, clarity, and empowerment. This sword cuts through illusions and frees us from the bonds of fear, doubt, and negativity. In Michael's hands, the Sword of Light becomes a beacon that reveals hidden truths and removes obstacles that hinder spiritual progress. To work with this powerful symbol is to invite Michael's assistance in transforming your life, shedding limitations, and stepping fully into your true strength.

The Sword of Light holds an energy of purity and courage, an invitation to embrace truth without compromise. Its light carries a frequency that dissolves any lower vibrations, breaking the chains of toxic attachments, unhealthy patterns, and past traumas. When you connect with Michael's sword, you are calling upon a force that can not only protect but transform, a force that clears the path forward, unburdening you from what no longer serves your highest self. To wield this sword is to accept Michael's guidance, allowing his energy to support you as you face challenges with confidence and integrity.

Before beginning your work with the Sword of Light, it is important to create a sacred space, a place free from distraction where you can focus on this connection. Start by cleansing your environment, using sage, incense, or simply visualizing a radiant light filling the space. This preparation clears away residual energies, setting the stage for the sword's powerful presence. The act of cleansing is itself a symbolic gesture, a way of removing barriers and opening yourself to receive the energy of Michael's sword.

With your space prepared, take a moment to center yourself through meditation. Close your eyes, take a few deep breaths, and feel your body relax. Visualize roots extending from your feet into the earth, grounding you, connecting you to the stability and strength of the world beneath. As you breathe, imagine a beam of pure white light descending from above, enveloping your body and filling you with peace. This light is the beginning of your connection to Michael's Sword of Light, a symbol of divine protection and truth.

In your mind's eye, begin to visualize the sword itself. See it as a magnificent, radiant blade, shimmering with a brilliant blue-white light. Its edge is sharp, gleaming with an intensity that speaks of truth and justice. Feel the sword's energy reaching out to you, inviting you to draw upon its strength. Imagine holding the sword in your hand, feeling its weight, its power, and its unwavering presence. This is Michael's gift to you, a tool that empowers you to release fears, doubts, and any illusions that have held you back.

As you hold this vision of the sword, consider any attachments or fears you wish to cut away. Perhaps it is a lingering insecurity, a toxic relationship, or a past event that continues to influence your present. Visualize these attachments as cords extending from your body, connecting you to these energies. These cords may appear as thin threads or thick, tangled ropes, but regardless of their appearance, they represent the ties that limit your freedom and drain your energy. They are the obstacles that keep you from stepping fully into your authentic self.

Raise the Sword of Light in your mind, and imagine its brilliant blade slicing through each cord with ease. With every cut, feel a surge of liberation, a lightness that fills the space where those attachments once existed. See the cords fall away, dissolving into pure light, their influence over you completely eradicated. Repeat this visualization until every cord is severed, until you feel completely free from those past ties. This act is not merely symbolic; it is a powerful ritual that invites Michael's assistance in releasing you from patterns that no longer serve you.

As you work with the sword, you may feel sensations of warmth or tingling, signs that Michael's energy is actively present. These sensations are the sword's energy moving through you, clearing away stagnant energies and aligning you with higher frequencies of courage and clarity. Trust in this experience, knowing that the Sword of Light is a tool not only of release but of empowerment. It allows you to reclaim parts of yourself that may have been lost to fear or doubt, reintegrating them into your being with a renewed sense of strength.

The Sword of Light can also be used to protect your energy, creating a boundary against negativity and harmful influences. To do this, visualize the sword in front of you, its blade glowing with a protective light. Imagine drawing a circle around yourself with the sword, its light forming a barrier that nothing harmful can penetrate. This circle becomes a shield, a sacred space where you are safe, secure, and untouched by any external negativity. In moments of vulnerability or uncertainty, this visualization provides a sanctuary, a place where Michael's protection surrounds and uplifts you.

This sword can be called upon in times of inner conflict as well. When facing difficult choices or navigating through complex emotions, visualize Michael's sword revealing the truth, cutting through any confusion or deception that clouds your mind. See the light of the sword illuminating your thoughts, casting out shadows, and bringing clarity. With the Sword of Light, you gain insight not only into your own motivations but also into the broader patterns at play, allowing you to make decisions from a place of wisdom and alignment with your highest self.

For those seeking deeper healing, the sword can also be used to release emotional wounds and traumas that linger in the heart and mind. Trauma often binds us to the past, creating patterns of fear and hesitation that prevent growth. Michael's sword has the power to cut through these emotional chains, freeing you from the grip of past pain. Hold the vision of the sword over your heart, allowing its light to penetrate deeply into the layers of hurt, fear, or anger. As you do this, breathe deeply, releasing any emotions that arise, letting the sword cleanse and transform them. Each breath becomes an act of release, each exhale a surrender of old wounds, allowing the sword's energy to heal and renew.

Another powerful way to incorporate the Sword of Light into your practice is through written intentions or affirmations. Write down what you wish to release or transform, such as "I release all fears that hold me back," or "I cut away self-doubt and embrace my inner strength." Hold this written intention in your hands, visualize the sword's light shining upon it, and imagine the words dissolving into pure light. By using the sword in this way, you are reinforcing your commitment to let go of limiting beliefs and to open yourself to new possibilities.

After working with the Sword of Light, take a moment to ground yourself, feeling your connection to the earth and to the present moment. Breathe deeply, allowing any residual energy to settle. Thank Michael for his presence, for the strength and clarity his sword has brought into your life. You may choose to close the session with a prayer or a gesture of gratitude, acknowledging the power of this sacred tool and the guidance it provides.

The Sword of Light is a tool you can return to whenever you feel burdened or in need of clarity. It is a reminder that Michael's protection and guidance are always available, that you are never without the means to free yourself from fear, doubt, or negativity. Working with this sword is an act of self-empowerment, a declaration that you are ready to walk your path with courage and integrity. Each time you hold the sword, you reaffirm your commitment to truth, to inner freedom, and to living as your highest self.

Over time, as you continue to work with Michael's sword, you may find that it becomes an integral part of your spiritual journey. Its presence will not only guide you but transform you, helping you shed the layers of limitation and uncover the radiant essence within. In wielding the Sword of Light, you are not merely invoking Michael's power but aligning with the strength and clarity that resides within your own soul.

In each challenge, in each moment of uncertainty, remember that this sword is there—a luminous tool, a protector, and a guide. It shines as a reminder of the light within you, a light that is forever protected, forever strong, and forever guided by the love and wisdom of Archangel Michael.

Chapter 7
Activating the Shield of Protection

The Shield of Protection associated with Archangel Michael is a powerful, unbreakable boundary of light that surrounds and fortifies the spirit. To invoke Michael's shield is to embrace a profound sense of security, an assurance that your energy, your thoughts, and your heart are safeguarded against negativity. This shield is not just a barrier; it is a field of divine energy, a sacred defense woven from light and strength. Working with Michael's shield allows you to walk through life with confidence, free from the shadows of fear and doubt. This shield is a gift, a form of spiritual armor that remains with you, as close as your heartbeat, as resilient as your own will.

The Shield of Protection begins with intention. It is activated not through force but through clarity of purpose and trust in Michael's presence. The first step to activating this shield is to focus your mind and heart on protection. Set the intention that you are safe, that you are surrounded by Michael's light, and that no harm can penetrate this sacred space. This intention acts as the key that unlocks the shield, transforming it from an abstract concept into a tangible field of energy that envelops and fortifies you.

Begin by finding a comfortable, quiet space where you can relax and center yourself. Close your eyes, take a few deep breaths, and allow the worries of the day to drift away. Imagine yourself sitting within a circle of light, a radiant field that separates you from the outer world. This light is the beginning of Michael's shield, a soft glow that fills the space around you with peace and safety. Let this light become brighter with each breath, intensifying as you focus your attention on it.

Visualize Michael standing before you, a powerful figure of protection, his shield glowing with a luminous blue light. This shield is not an ordinary shield; it is a divine tool, a living energy that adapts to your needs. See Michael extending this shield toward you, his intention clear and unwavering: to protect, to guard, to keep you safe. In this moment, feel his presence filling the space, a tangible force of compassion and strength that envelops you.

As you continue to visualize, see Michael placing this shield directly in front of you, a barrier that emanates strength and protection. Imagine it expanding around you, forming a dome or sphere of light that encloses you completely. This shield is not rigid; it is fluid and adaptable, a living energy that adjusts to the needs of the moment. Visualize it surrounding you, creating a space where only light and love can enter. This is your sacred boundary, an energetic armor that guards against any intrusion of fear, negativity, or harmful intent.

To deepen this connection, imagine yourself touching the shield, feeling its energy with your hands. The surface of the shield may feel warm, pulsating with a vibrant, calming energy. This touch affirms the shield's presence, reminding you that it is real, that it exists in both the visible and invisible realms. Feel the strength of this shield resonating through your entire being, a reminder that you are protected, supported, and aligned with Michael's energy.

To activate the shield fully, bring your focus to your heart. Michael's protection is strongest when it aligns with the purity of the heart's intention. Breathe deeply, letting the breath flow in and out of your heart center. With each breath, imagine the shield growing stronger, its light intensifying, its power solidifying. In this moment, affirm that this shield is a permanent part of your energy field, that it is not just a temporary defense but a constant presence that remains with you. You may say silently or aloud, "Archangel Michael, I call upon your shield of protection.

Surround me in your light, guard me from all harm, and keep my heart safe and strong."

At this point, you may notice sensations within your body—warmth in the chest, tingling in the hands, or a gentle pressure around you. These feelings are signs that Michael's shield is fully activated, that his energy is merging with your own. Allow yourself to relax into this sensation, trusting in the strength of the shield and in Michael's commitment to your safety. This is a time of pure receptivity, a moment to let go of fears and to embrace the security of divine protection.

Michael's shield is especially powerful in situations where you feel vulnerable, whether emotionally, mentally, or physically. When you face environments or interactions that feel challenging or draining, remember that this shield is with you. Visualize it around you, a constant, protective presence that keeps negative energies at bay. You may choose to visualize the shield in various forms, adapting it to the circumstances: a circle of light, a bubble, or even a cloak that wraps around you. Michael's shield is versatile, and its power lies in its ability to meet your unique needs.

In addition to shielding against external negativity, Michael's shield can help you navigate inner turmoil. Our own thoughts and emotions can sometimes create obstacles, filling our minds with self-doubt or anxiety. When this happens, imagine Michael's shield around your mind, creating a space where only truth and positivity can reside. Let the shield act as a filter, allowing only empowering thoughts and feelings to enter. This practice can be particularly helpful in moments of self-reflection or meditation, creating a sacred mental space that is free from distractions and self-criticism.

To anchor Michael's shield in your daily life, consider using physical symbols as reminders. Wearing a pendant or carrying a small stone, like obsidian or black tourmaline, can reinforce the sense of protection. These stones hold grounding and shielding energies, amplifying the shield's presence throughout the day. Each time you touch this object, let it remind you of Michael's shield, of the light and protection that surrounds you.

Another powerful way to work with Michael's shield is to visualize it surrounding not only yourself but also your loved ones, home, and any space that feels in need of protection. As you visualize, see the shield expanding, covering those you care about, forming a protective dome over them. Picture it glowing with Michael's blue light, a guardian force that repels negativity and danger. This expanded shield acts as an energy field that extends Michael's protection to those you hold dear, a silent prayer for their safety and well-being.

Michael's shield can also be called upon during sleep, a vulnerable time when our defenses are lowered. Before going to bed, take a few moments to activate the shield around you, envisioning it as a cocoon of light that surrounds your body. This practice creates a barrier against negative influences that may try to enter your energy field during the night. Visualize the shield growing stronger as you sleep, reinforcing your energy and ensuring a peaceful, restorative rest. If you have dreams that feel unsettling, visualize Michael's shield surrounding you, turning any dark images into light, transforming the dream space into a place of peace.

For those who work in environments filled with stress or tension, Michael's shield can serve as a valuable daily tool. When entering such spaces, take a moment to visualize the shield around you, a protective layer that prevents external negativity from entering your energy field. Imagine it filtering the energy around you, allowing only positive vibrations to reach you. This practice can be particularly empowering for those in caregiving or high-stress professions, providing a buffer that keeps you grounded and centered.

Through continued practice, Michael's shield becomes a natural part of your life. The more you work with it, the stronger its presence becomes, until it feels as though this shield is always with you, woven into your energy field. The boundary it creates is both protective and empowering, allowing you to engage fully with the world while remaining safe and secure. This shield is not merely a defense; it is a constant reminder of Michael's guardianship, a symbol that you are never alone, that you are always watched over by divine forces.

When you encounter challenges, remember that Michael's shield is there. In moments of fear or uncertainty, visualize this shield around you, feel its strength, and know that you are protected. The shield does not only guard you; it empowers you to face life with confidence, to walk forward with the knowledge that you are safe, resilient, and supported. Each time you activate the shield, you reaffirm this protection, anchoring Michael's energy into your heart, mind, and spirit.

Michael's shield is more than a boundary against harm; it is a sacred space that enables you to explore your own truth, to live fully and without fear. Within this shield, you find the freedom to be yourself, to pursue your dreams, and to engage with life from a place of security and peace. It is an invitation to walk your path without hesitation, to live with courage, knowing that you are forever protected by the light of Archangel Michael.

In embracing this shield, you invite Michael's strength to merge with your own. The boundary it creates is also a gateway, allowing his protection to enter your life fully, deeply, and permanently. With each use, you deepen your connection to his energy, allowing his light to guide and guard you through all of life's trials. The shield becomes a part of your spiritual armor, a reminder of the strength that lies within and the divine support that surrounds you.

As you walk forward, carry this shield with you. Trust in its power, feel its presence, and know that with Michael by your side, you are safe, whole, and free. This shield is your sanctuary, your strength, a gift of divine protection that will forever light your path.

Chapter 8
Balancing with the Divine Scale

Archangel Michael's Divine Scale is a symbol of balance, justice, and alignment with the highest truth. In the spiritual journey, balance is the foundation upon which wisdom and clarity rest. The Divine Scale is a reminder that true strength is found not in extremes but in the harmony of opposites—the merging of power and peace, courage and compassion, truth and understanding. Working with Michael's scale invites a process of introspection and alignment, a way to measure and adjust one's energies, intentions, and actions to a state of balance that resonates with the soul's highest purpose.

Michael's scale is not simply a tool of judgment; it is a mirror, reflecting the true state of one's inner and outer life. Through this scale, we are invited to examine not only the choices we make but also the motivations that guide them, weighing our intentions with honesty and clarity. This practice of balance calls for a commitment to truth, a willingness to see things as they are, without illusion. By aligning with Michael's scale, we are granted the courage to confront our inner imbalances and the wisdom to make choices that bring us closer to harmony with our true selves.

To begin working with the Divine Scale, create a space of stillness and reflection. Sit in a comfortable position, close your eyes, and focus on your breath. Imagine yourself in a vast, open space—a sacred space beyond time and place. In this setting, visualize Michael standing before you, a figure of strength and serenity, holding a golden scale that glows with a gentle, otherworldly light. This scale is balanced, each side perfectly aligned, a reflection of divine order. Its presence evokes a sense of peace, a reminder that in balance, there is harmony, and in harmony, there is truth.

As you observe the scale, feel its energy extending toward you, inviting you to place upon it anything that feels out of alignment. Think about areas in your life where imbalance may exist. Perhaps you have been overextending yourself, neglecting rest or personal boundaries. Or perhaps an emotional weight, such as anger or regret, has tilted your inner scale, pulling you away from peace. With each of these thoughts, visualize them as objects or symbols, and gently place them on one side of the scale in your mind. As you do so, feel a release, a willingness to confront these imbalances openly, without judgment.

With each item you place upon the scale, take a moment to breathe deeply, allowing any resistance to dissolve. The Divine Scale is not here to punish or judge; it is here to reveal, to illuminate the path to balance. As the scale shifts, watch it respond, adjusting to the weight of each energy, each thought, each intention. Feel Michael's presence beside you, his strength and wisdom enveloping you, providing the courage to confront any truths that may arise. He stands with you, a steady and compassionate guide, helping you see your life with clarity.

After placing these weights upon the scale, turn your attention to the other side—the side of balance, harmony, and peace. Here, visualize qualities that you wish to bring into your life to restore balance. Perhaps it is patience, forgiveness, self-compassion, or the courage to set healthier boundaries. Imagine these qualities as radiant symbols of light, and place them upon the other side of the scale, one by one. With each addition, feel a lightness, a sense of alignment that brings the scale closer to balance. This is not a forced equilibrium; it is a natural alignment that honors both your needs and your values.

As you continue, notice how each placement on the scale affects your energy. Perhaps you feel a subtle shift within—a release of tension, an emergence of clarity. The Divine Scale reflects not only the state of your outer life but the alignment of your inner world. As you bring these qualities into balance, you may experience a profound sense of harmony, as though the scale is not simply an external tool but a mirror of your soul. With Michael by your side, feel the strength to let go of any attachments, fears, or beliefs that no longer serve your journey.

The process of balancing with the Divine Scale is not a single act; it is a practice, a daily invitation to examine the inner and outer elements of your life with honesty and compassion. You may wish to revisit this exercise periodically, especially during times of change or challenge, to recalibrate and ensure that your path remains true to your highest intentions. Each time you return, the scale becomes easier to work with, as though it remembers your energies, understanding the nuances of your journey and aligning with your progress.

Michael's Divine Scale can also be used as a guide for making decisions. When faced with a choice, whether large or small, visualize the scale in your mind and place the options on either side. Observe how each option affects the balance. Does one side feel heavier, weighed down by doubt or fear? Does the other feel lighter, aligned with your truth and values? By working with the scale in this way, you allow your inner wisdom to speak, guided by Michael's energy toward choices that align with balance and integrity. This practice cultivates discernment, helping you recognize the choices that support your growth and well-being.

The Divine Scale also invites reflection on the balance of giving and receiving. Life is an exchange of energy, a flow that must remain balanced to sustain harmony. If you find yourself constantly giving, carrying others' burdens without replenishing your own energy, the scale will reflect this imbalance. Likewise, if you are in a period of receiving but not sharing your light with others, the scale encourages you to find ways to give back, to contribute to the harmony around you. By honoring this balance, you enter a rhythm that flows naturally, where you are nourished and also nourish, a state of true equilibrium.

Through the Divine Scale, Michael also encourages the balance of action and reflection. In our world, there is often pressure to constantly act, to be in motion, to achieve and accomplish. Yet the soul requires moments of stillness, times of reflection to integrate experiences and draw wisdom from them. If your life feels tilted toward constant activity, use the scale to bring in moments of quiet, times when you simply listen, rest, and allow insights to arise naturally. This balance of doing and being creates a harmonious rhythm, a life that honors both the physical and spiritual needs.

Working with the Divine Scale can also reveal imbalances in thought patterns and beliefs. Sometimes, we carry beliefs that weigh us down, inherited ideas about success, worth, or happiness that do not truly align with our soul's path. By placing these beliefs on the scale, we can see their impact, feel their weight, and decide if they are worth keeping. Michael's scale invites you to replace these heavy beliefs with those that lift you, affirming ideas that resonate with your highest self. This process frees you from old patterns, allowing you to live with a lightness and authenticity that reflects your truest values.

Another aspect of balance that the Divine Scale illuminates is the harmony between self-care and service to others. Michael's path is one of devotion and protection, yet he teaches that true service requires a balance of giving to oneself and to others. When your energy is depleted, the scale will show the imbalance, a reminder that nurturing yourself is essential to offering true support to those around you. By cultivating this balance, you honor both your personal needs and your commitment to others, creating a life of sustainable service rooted in love and respect.

At the end of your work with the Divine Scale, take a moment to observe how you feel. Notice any shifts in your body, mind, or emotions. Often, this practice brings a sense of peace, a lightness that reflects the alignment of your energies. Offer gratitude to Michael, acknowledging his presence and guidance, for he stands not as a distant figure but as an ally who walks beside you, helping you find your way to balance and truth.

As you move forward, carry the lessons of the Divine Scale with you. Allow it to become a part of your daily life, a silent guide that helps you weigh each decision, each action, and each thought. This balance is not rigid; it is a living, dynamic harmony that adapts and flows with you. It allows you to engage fully with life, grounded in a sense of inner peace and alignment.

Through the Divine Scale, you learn to walk the path with grace, neither leaning too far in any direction nor held back by extremes. Michael's scale becomes a tool not just of balance but of liberation, freeing you from the pulls of the external world, grounding you in the clarity of your soul's truth. This balance is your strength, your sanctuary, a place of unwavering stability where you can stand with Michael, aligned with the divine will, aligned with your highest self.

Each time you work with the Divine Scale, you deepen your connection to Michael's energy, allowing his presence to guide you through life's complexities with wisdom and grace. This practice of balance becomes a source of strength, a foundation upon which you build a life of authenticity, courage, and peace. With Michael's scale, you are reminded that true balance is not an absence of movement but a harmony of forces, a state where the soul can breathe freely, grounded in love, aligned with truth, walking with Michael's light always beside you.

Chapter 9
Transmuting with the Blue Flame

The Blue Flame of Archangel Michael is one of the most powerful symbols of spiritual transformation. It is a flame that does not burn but purifies, a force that transmutes darkness into light and fear into courage. Working with the Blue Flame is an invitation to release, cleanse, and renew, shedding layers of negativity and allowing the soul's true essence to shine through. This flame is Michael's gift of transmutation, a process that not only purifies but elevates, turning pain into wisdom, anger into compassion, and doubt into faith. To embrace the Blue Flame is to embrace transformation at the deepest level, inviting a divine energy that flows from the heart of Michael himself.

The Blue Flame, as it is often visualized, glows with an intense sapphire or cobalt hue, a color that radiates a vibration of strength and peace. This flame is not merely a symbol; it is a living energy that connects directly to Michael's power, bridging the realms of the physical and spiritual to initiate profound changes within. When called upon, the Blue Flame becomes a force of divine alchemy, burning away the impurities within our hearts, minds, and energy fields, leaving only truth and clarity in its wake. It is a sacred fire that cleanses not by destruction but by transformation, allowing the soul to emerge renewed and strengthened.

To begin working with the Blue Flame, find a quiet space where you can sit in peace and stillness. Close your eyes, take a few deep breaths, and center yourself. As you inhale, imagine drawing in Michael's energy, filling your body with a gentle yet powerful light. Exhale any tensions or worries, releasing them to the earth. Continue this breathing, allowing it to bring you into a deep state of relaxation, a place where you are open and receptive to the energy of the Blue Flame.

In your mind's eye, visualize a flame beginning to form in front of you. See it flickering gently, glowing with an intense blue light that grows brighter with each breath. This is the Blue Flame of Archangel Michael, a flame that holds within it the power to transform and uplift. Feel its warmth, a warmth that is comforting rather than overwhelming, and let it draw you in. Imagine this flame expanding, filling the space around you, surrounding you with a radiant, protective glow. This is the space where transmutation begins, where you are free to release anything that no longer serves your journey.

With the Blue Flame before you, think of any emotions, thoughts, or energies you wish to transform. Perhaps there is a lingering fear that holds you back, a past hurt that weighs on your heart, or a pattern of doubt that clouds your mind. Visualize these energies as dark, heavy shapes or symbols, things that carry the weight of old energy. One by one, place each of these symbols into the Blue Flame, watching as the flame engulfs them, its light dissolving the darkness. As these shapes enter the flame, see them transform into light, becoming weightless, pure, and clear.

As you release these energies, notice any sensations in your body. You may feel a lightness, a warmth, or a tingling sensation as the Blue Flame clears away the stagnant energy. This is the power of transmutation, a process that not only removes but transforms, allowing what was once a source of heaviness to become a source of strength. Michael's Blue Flame works deeply, reaching into the hidden corners of your being, illuminating shadows and bringing them to light. Trust in this process, knowing that the flame is guided by Michael's wisdom and love, working in harmony with your soul's highest good.

The Blue Flame can also be used as a tool for healing past wounds. Trauma and pain can leave imprints on our energy fields, lingering as shadows that influence our thoughts, emotions, and actions. To release these imprints, bring to mind any past event or memory that feels unresolved, something that still carries an emotional charge. Hold this memory in your mind, and visualize it as a shape or color. Place it into the Blue Flame, watching as the flame envelops it, transforming it from darkness to light. As the memory dissolves, feel a sense of release, a freedom from the grip of the past, as Michael's flame purifies and heals this part of your story.

When working with the Blue Flame, it is important to set an intention. The intention might be as simple as, "I release all that no longer serves my highest good," or "I open myself to healing and transformation." This intention acts as a guide, directing the flame's energy toward your desired outcome, allowing Michael's power to work with clarity and purpose. Each time you set an intention, you align yourself with the flame's energy, creating a space where transformation can happen freely and naturally.

To deepen your connection to the Blue Flame, visualize it entering your body, filling you from the inside out. Imagine the flame at the center of your being, expanding with each breath, its light illuminating every part of you. See it moving through your heart, dissolving any old pain, opening you to love and compassion. Feel it moving through your mind, clearing away doubts, fears, and limiting beliefs, creating space for clarity and peace. Let the flame flow through every cell, purifying and energizing you, aligning you with Michael's strength and resilience.

The Blue Flame is also a powerful tool for clearing your surroundings. Just as it cleanses your energy field, it can also purify spaces, removing stagnant or negative energies from your home or workspace. To do this, imagine the Blue Flame expanding outward, filling the room, moving into every corner and shadowed space. Visualize it clearing away any lingering energy that does not align with love and light, leaving the space feeling fresh, vibrant, and peaceful. This process creates an environment that supports your well-being, a sanctuary where Michael's energy can be felt and appreciated.

During times of stress or emotional turmoil, call upon the Blue Flame to bring peace and balance. Imagine it surrounding you like a cloak, its light absorbing any anxiety, anger, or frustration. Feel the flame working gently but powerfully, transmuting these emotions into calm and resilience. This visualization can be done at any time, even in the midst of difficult situations, to help you stay centered and aligned with Michael's protection.

Over time, working with the Blue Flame becomes a practice of renewal. Each time you return to it, you deepen your connection to Michael's transformative energy, allowing it to shape and strengthen you. The flame's power is not limited to moments of release; it can also be a source of inspiration and creativity. When you feel blocked or stagnant, imagine the Blue Flame within you, a spark of divine energy that ignites your passion and creativity, helping you move forward with confidence and purpose.

In addition to visualization, you may find it helpful to incorporate physical symbols of the Blue Flame into your space. A blue candle, a sapphire stone, or even a simple piece of blue cloth can serve as reminders of this energy. When you light the candle or hold the stone, let it reconnect you with the Blue Flame, allowing you to feel its presence in a tangible way. These objects become focal points, anchoring the energy of transmutation in your daily life, a physical link to Michael's transformative power.

The Blue Flame also serves as a reminder of your own inner light, a symbol of the strength and purity that lies within each soul. As you work with this flame, you awaken parts of yourself that may have been hidden or forgotten, qualities of courage, love, and wisdom that are as much a part of you as they are of Michael's essence. This process of awakening is the true purpose of transmutation—not merely to release but to uncover the soul's fullest potential, allowing it to shine with its own radiant light.

At the end of each session with the Blue Flame, take a moment to offer gratitude to Archangel Michael. Thank him for his presence, for the gift of transformation, and for the courage to embrace change. Close the session by visualizing the flame gently dimming, leaving behind a deep sense of peace and clarity. Know that the flame's work continues even after the visualization, that its energy remains within you, supporting your growth and healing.

As you go about your daily life, remember that the Blue Flame is always with you. In moments of challenge or doubt, visualize it glowing within your heart, a constant source of strength and renewal. This flame is not separate from you; it is a part of your spirit, a reminder of the resilience and purity that define your true self. Each time you work with it, you align more deeply with Michael's energy, inviting his wisdom and strength to guide you on your path.

Through the Blue Flame, you become a vessel for transformation, carrying within you the power to transmute negativity into light, to turn fear into courage, to move forward with clarity and grace. This flame is your ally, your guide, a gift from Michael that empowers you to live in alignment with your highest self. With the Blue Flame beside you, you walk a path of light, forever supported, forever transformed, and forever connected to the strength and love of Archangel Michael.

Chapter 10
Integrating Michael's Attributes

Integrating the spiritual attributes of Archangel Michael is a path of transformation, a journey that involves embodying the qualities he represents—courage, justice, protection, truth, and unwavering faith. Michael's presence is one of action and commitment, a force that inspires strength in those who seek his guidance. To integrate these attributes is to bring his divine energy into the core of your being, allowing his qualities to shape your thoughts, actions, and interactions. In doing so, you become not only a recipient of his protection but a reflection of his light in the world, a channel through which his virtues can flourish.

This integration is a practice, a daily commitment to cultivate and embody the qualities Michael exemplifies. It requires both intention and self-awareness, a willingness to observe your inner state and make conscious choices that align with his energy. Each of Michael's attributes represents a facet of the soul's highest potential, and by nurturing these qualities within yourself, you deepen your connection to his presence. This path is not one of imitation but of resonance, an alignment of your soul's essence with the divine virtues that Michael brings forth.

To begin integrating Michael's attributes, start with **courage**, the foundation of his energy. Courage is more than fearlessness; it is the strength to move forward even when fear arises, a willingness to embrace truth regardless of the discomfort it may bring. In moments of self-doubt or hesitation, call upon Michael's courage. Close your eyes, take a deep breath, and imagine his energy surrounding you like a shield of blue light.

Feel his courage merging with your own, filling you with a calm resolve that transcends fear. With each experience that challenges your resolve, let this courage guide you, a reminder that true strength lies not in avoiding difficulty but in facing it with an open heart.

Michael's courage invites you to step fully into your truth. Living in alignment with your truth requires self-honesty, a willingness to acknowledge both strengths and weaknesses without judgment. This attribute calls for constant introspection, a gentle but firm examination of your inner world. When facing difficult decisions or moments of uncertainty, pause to ask yourself: "What is true for me in this moment?" Allow Michael's energy to guide you as you seek your own authentic answer. The truth may not always be easy, but with Michael's courage, you find the strength to honor it.

Justice is another vital attribute of Michael's energy, representing fairness, integrity, and respect for all beings. In every thought, word, and deed, justice calls you to consider the impact of your actions on yourself and others. This attribute aligns with the idea of divine order, the understanding that each choice contributes to the greater harmony or disharmony in the world. To embody Michael's sense of justice, practice mindfulness in your interactions. Listen carefully, speak truthfully, and act with kindness. Justice does not seek to punish but to restore balance, a balance that respects the well-being of all. By cultivating this quality, you bring Michael's sense of fairness into your life, creating harmony and respect in all that you do.

When faced with conflict, call upon Michael's justice to guide you toward resolution. Imagine his scales of balance, weighing each aspect of the situation. Reflect on the perspectives of others involved, and seek a solution that honors truth and equity. Justice in this sense is an act of love, a dedication to harmony and respect. It requires patience and compassion, qualities that elevate your interactions and align your life with the principles of divine fairness. By embodying this attribute, you become a source of balance, a presence that radiates peace and understanding.

Protection is one of Michael's most recognized attributes, a quality that resonates deeply with those who seek his presence. This protection is not only physical but also emotional and spiritual, a boundary that guards against negative influences and harmful energies. To integrate this quality, cultivate boundaries that honor your well-being. These boundaries are not walls but spaces of respect, a way to protect your energy while remaining open and compassionate. Michael's protection encourages you to be discerning, to know when to say "no" and when to distance yourself from energies that disrupt your peace.

Visualize Michael's shield surrounding you, a radiant field of light that protects without isolating. Feel his energy reinforcing your boundaries, a strength that allows you to interact with others from a place of confidence and clarity. As you embody this protection, you create a safe space for yourself and those around you. This boundary enables you to give from a place of wholeness rather than depletion, a protection that nourishes both yourself and those in your presence. By holding this space, you become a vessel of Michael's protective energy, a source of safety and stability for others.

Faith is a cornerstone of Michael's presence, a quality that holds unwavering trust in the divine plan and the resilience to move forward despite uncertainty. Faith is the inner assurance that no matter the circumstances, you are guided and supported by a power greater than yourself. This attribute allows you to surrender control, to let go of fear and doubt, and to trust in the process of life. To cultivate faith, practice moments of surrender. In times of challenge or doubt, release your worries to Michael, envisioning them as threads of light that he carries to the divine. Feel his energy lifting the weight from your heart, reminding you that you are never alone.

Faith encourages you to walk your path with confidence, trusting that each step is part of a larger journey. Even when outcomes are unclear, faith allows you to move forward with purpose and resilience. This faith is not passive; it is an active trust, a willingness to engage with life fully, knowing that every experience holds meaning. By embodying this quality, you align yourself with the flow of divine wisdom, becoming a channel for grace, strength, and purpose.

Compassion is another powerful attribute of Michael's energy, an empathy that radiates from his strength and courage. Michael's compassion is not sentimental; it is a fierce and unwavering love that seeks to uplift and protect. To integrate this quality, cultivate compassion not only for others but also for yourself. Compassion begins with self-acceptance, a willingness to see oneself with kindness and patience. In times of self-criticism or doubt, call upon Michael's compassion, allowing his gentle energy to fill your heart. Imagine him placing a hand over your heart, a warm presence that dissolves judgment and replaces it with love.

As you nurture compassion within, extend this quality outward. In your interactions, listen with an open heart, seek to understand rather than to judge, and offer kindness even in difficult situations. Compassion does not mean accepting harmful behavior; it means seeing the humanity in others and responding with empathy and respect. Michael's compassion guides you to love without attachment, to give without expectation, creating connections that are grounded in mutual respect and understanding. This compassion is a source of healing, a balm that soothes both the giver and the receiver.

Finally, integrating Michael's **wisdom** is a process of aligning your thoughts and actions with higher truth. Wisdom is more than knowledge; it is the application of truth in a way that uplifts and empowers. Michael's wisdom encourages discernment, an ability to see beyond surface appearances and understand the deeper patterns at play. To cultivate this wisdom, practice introspection, a habit of looking within to seek understanding and insight. Wisdom emerges from reflection, from moments of stillness where you can hear the quiet voice of intuition guiding you.

In moments of uncertainty, ask for Michael's guidance, and listen with an open mind. This wisdom often comes as subtle insights, a quiet clarity that feels true without explanation. Trust these impressions, allowing them to inform your actions and decisions. By integrating Michael's wisdom, you learn to navigate life with grace, moving forward with a sense of purpose and understanding. Wisdom allows you to live authentically, to act with integrity, and to align your life with the highest good.

The process of integrating Michael's attributes is a path of spiritual growth, a journey that deepens your connection to his presence with each step. Each attribute—courage, justice, protection, faith, compassion, and wisdom—offers a unique facet of his energy, a quality that elevates your life and aligns you with divine purpose. By embodying these qualities, you not only strengthen your bond with Michael but also become a beacon of his light in the world.

This integration is not a destination but a practice, a daily commitment to live with intention and awareness. As you walk this path, you may find that these attributes emerge naturally, that they become second nature, woven into the fabric of your being. In moments of difficulty, remember that Michael's presence is always with you, a constant source of support and strength. Through his guidance, you are empowered to live with courage, integrity, and love.

As you embody Michael's attributes, you transform not only your own life but also the lives of those around you. Your presence becomes a source of peace, a reflection of the qualities that Michael represents. You become a channel for his light, a vessel through which his energy flows, bringing hope, protection, and love to all who cross your path. This is the gift of integration—a life aligned with truth, a heart open to love, a spirit guided by the light of Archangel Michael.

Each day, reaffirm your connection to Michael, inviting his energy to merge with your own. Let his courage, justice, protection, faith, compassion, and wisdom be your guide, a foundation upon which you build a life of purpose and grace. In this integration, you find not only guidance but transformation, a journey that brings you ever closer to the divine essence within. Through Michael's attributes, you walk forward in strength, a reflection of his light, a beacon of his love, a testament to his unwavering presence in your life.

Chapter 11
Angelic Initiation Ritual

The Angelic Initiation Ritual with Archangel Michael is a sacred and profound ceremony, a rite that opens the soul to a deeper, committed relationship with the archangel. This initiation marks the beginning of a spiritual journey where Michael's guidance, protection, and wisdom become an integral part of your life. Through this ritual, you dedicate yourself to a path of courage, truth, and spiritual growth, aligning your intentions and energies with those of the archangel. The initiation is a symbolic crossing of a threshold, a commitment to honor the qualities Michael embodies and to walk in alignment with his divine light.

The initiation ritual is a transformative experience, a calling forth of your highest self, and an invitation for Michael's presence to become woven into your spiritual path. Preparing for this ceremony involves purifying your body, mind, and spirit, creating a space of openness and readiness to receive Michael's light. The ritual does not only mark a new chapter in your journey; it invites a sacred bond, a partnership that supports you as you move forward on a path of protection, clarity, and divine purpose.

Before beginning, it's important to approach the ritual with a clear heart and focused mind. Spend some time reflecting on your intentions, asking yourself why you wish to deepen your connection with Michael. Are you seeking his guidance for a specific purpose? Do you desire a stronger sense of protection or wish to embody his qualities of courage and justice? Whatever your reasons, let them resonate deeply within you, allowing them to settle in your heart as clear and sincere intentions. These intentions become the foundation of your initiation, the spiritual anchor that aligns your energy with Michael's light.

The preparation for the initiation ritual begins with a period of purification. This is a time to cleanse not only your physical body but also your emotional and mental space. Consider taking a ritual bath or shower, infused with salts or herbs, such as lavender, frankincense, or sage, which are known for their purifying properties. As you wash, imagine the water carrying away any negativity, doubt, or fear, leaving you refreshed, renewed, and ready to receive Michael's energy. Allow yourself to be present in this moment of cleansing, feeling gratitude for this process of renewal.

Next, prepare a sacred space where the initiation will take place. This space should be free from distractions, a place where you feel safe, peaceful, and focused. Place objects that resonate with Michael's energy within this space, such as a blue or white candle, a piece of angelite or lapis lazuli, or an image of Michael himself. These items serve as focal points, grounding the ritual in the physical world and amplifying your connection to the archangel. Light the candle as a symbol of Michael's presence, its flame a representation of the divine light you are about to welcome into your heart.

When you are ready to begin, sit comfortably within this space, and close your eyes. Take several deep breaths, grounding yourself and centering your mind. As you breathe, feel your body relax, each exhalation releasing any tension or lingering thoughts. Visualize roots extending from your feet into the earth, anchoring you, connecting you to the stability and strength of the earth below. At the same time, feel a soft, gentle light descending from above, entering through the crown of your head, filling your body with warmth and peace.

When you feel centered, call upon Michael, inviting his presence to join you. Speak aloud or in your mind, saying: "Archangel Michael, guardian of truth and light, I call upon you now. I open my heart to your guidance, your protection, and your wisdom. I ask for your presence in this sacred initiation, that I may walk the path of courage, truth, and divine purpose." As you speak, visualize Michael standing before you, his figure radiant with light, a presence that fills the space with peace and strength.

In this moment, allow yourself to feel his energy—an aura of protection, compassion, and unwavering courage. Michael's presence is powerful yet gentle, a force that both grounds and elevates. Imagine his hand reaching toward you, offering you the strength to stand fully in your truth, to let go of fear, and to embrace your path with confidence. Feel his light surrounding you, forming a sphere of protection, a shield that guards your spirit as you move into this new phase of spiritual growth.

To symbolize your commitment, place your hand over your heart and speak your intention aloud. For example, you might say, "I dedicate myself to a path of truth, courage, and love, with Archangel Michael as my guide and protector. I commit to embodying his light in my thoughts, words, and actions, to serve the highest good, and to walk in alignment with divine will." Feel these words resonate within you, anchoring your commitment, each syllable a pledge that unites your soul with Michael's energy.

The next step in the ritual is to receive Michael's blessing. Visualize him placing a hand on your head or heart, his light flowing into you, filling you with strength and courage. This blessing is not only a gift but a transfer of energy, a merging of Michael's presence with your own. Feel his qualities of protection, justice, and clarity infusing your being, a powerful force that lifts you, aligning you with your highest self. As this energy flows through you, know that you are being prepared, strengthened, and empowered for the path ahead.

Now, imagine Michael extending his sword of light toward you. This sword is a symbol of truth, purity, and divine protection. See its blade glowing with a vibrant blue flame, a light that cuts through all illusions, fears, and doubts. Michael offers this sword to you, not as a weapon, but as a tool of clarity and empowerment. In your mind, reach out to accept this sword, feeling its energy merge with your own. With this act, you are accepting Michael's guidance, his strength, and his protection, making his light a permanent part of your journey.

In the next stage, visualize a blue flame within your heart, a flame that represents Michael's essence now residing within you. This flame is a source of strength, a constant reminder of his presence, a light that guides you through any darkness. As you breathe, feel this flame growing stronger, filling your entire being with its radiant glow. This light is now a part of you, a permanent source of courage, truth, and protection that you carry with you wherever you go.

To complete the ritual, take a moment of silence to integrate Michael's energy within. Sit with this feeling, allowing the light to settle, becoming one with your own energy. In this stillness, know that you are now connected to Michael's presence on a deeper level, that his guidance and protection are woven into the fabric of your spirit. This connection is unbreakable, a bond that grows stronger with each choice you make in alignment with his virtues.

When you feel ready, offer gratitude to Michael. Say, "Thank you, Archangel Michael, for your presence, for your protection, and for this sacred initiation. May I walk my path with courage, truth, and love, guided by your light and strengthened by your spirit." As you speak these words, visualize Michael smiling, his energy surrounding you in a warm embrace, his light a shield that protects you as you move forward.

Finally, close the ritual by visualizing the sacred space gently fading, the light around you dimming, leaving only the blue flame within your heart as a reminder of this initiation. Know that this flame is a permanent connection, a source of strength and guidance that will remain with you throughout your life. When you open your eyes, feel a renewed sense of purpose, a feeling of peace and confidence that reflects the power of Michael's presence within you.

This initiation is more than a single moment; it is a gateway, a beginning of a deeper, lifelong relationship with

Archangel Michael. Each time you call upon him, each time you embody his virtues, you honor this initiation, strengthening the bond between your soul and his light. This ritual is a foundation upon which you can build, a sacred pledge that guides your thoughts, actions, and intentions as you walk your spiritual path.

As you carry Michael's energy forward, remember that you are a vessel of his light, a reflection of his strength, and a testament to his protection. This initiation ritual marks the start of a new chapter, a journey where you are never alone, forever guided by the presence of Archangel Michael, forever aligned with his divine purpose.

Chapter 12
Meditating with Michael's Presence

Meditating with the presence of Archangel Michael is a practice that draws his energy close, allowing his guidance, protection, and wisdom to fill your mind and heart. This form of meditation opens a space where Michael's light can be felt tangibly, deepening your spiritual connection with him and inviting a profound peace that radiates from his essence. Through meditation, you are not merely calling on Michael but aligning with his energy in a way that fosters clarity, inner strength, and a fortified sense of purpose.

Meditation is a pathway, a bridge to realms beyond the visible, and when you attune yourself to Michael in this way, you create a sacred meeting ground where his guidance can reach you with clarity and ease. This practice invites his energy directly into your heart and mind, creating a space of communion where words are not necessary and presence speaks louder than thought. Meditating with Michael's presence requires openness and an inner willingness to receive, to allow his light to guide you to deeper places within yourself, illuminating truths that may otherwise remain hidden.

To prepare for meditation with Michael, choose a quiet space where you can relax without interruptions. This space should be comfortable and peaceful, a place where you feel safe and receptive. If you wish, light a blue or white candle as a symbol of Michael's presence, letting the flame represent his divine light that will guide you through the meditation. You may also place a crystal associated with Michael, such as lapis lazuli or angelite, nearby to ground his energy in the physical realm.

Begin by sitting comfortably, either cross-legged on the floor or on a chair with your feet planted firmly on the ground. Close your eyes and take a few deep, calming breaths, allowing each exhale to release any tension, stress, or thoughts that may be occupying your mind. As you breathe, focus on creating a rhythm, letting each breath flow in and out naturally. With each breath, feel yourself relaxing more deeply, your body becoming grounded, your mind quieting into stillness.

Once you feel centered, bring your awareness to your heart center, the place where you will invite Michael's energy to dwell during this meditation. Visualize a small, glowing light in the center of your chest, a light that pulses gently with each heartbeat. This light is your own divine essence, a point of connection to the spiritual realms. See it growing brighter with each breath, expanding to fill your chest with warmth and peace. This inner light is the doorway through which Michael's energy will enter, a sacred space within you that holds the potential for profound transformation.

With your focus on your heart, call upon Michael, inviting his presence to join you in this meditation. In your mind or aloud, say, "Archangel Michael, I invite your presence to be with me in this moment. Surround me with your light, your peace, and your guidance. May I feel your presence deeply and open myself fully to your protection and wisdom." As you speak these words, imagine your heart opening like a flower, unfolding petal by petal, creating a space of love and receptivity for Michael's energy.

Begin to visualize a powerful, blue light descending from above, a vibrant, sapphire-blue radiance that fills the space around you. This light is the essence of Michael's presence, a pure and protective energy that brings peace to all it touches. See this blue light surrounding you, forming a cocoon of divine protection, a shield that blocks all negative influences and fills your space with love and serenity. Allow yourself to feel this light, sensing its warmth, its strength, and its steady, unwavering energy.

Now, see this blue light entering your heart center, merging with the light that is already there. As these two lights combine, feel your heart expanding, filling with a profound sense of peace and strength. Michael's presence is now within you, a part of your own energy. Feel his strength and courage flowing into you, grounding you in a deep sense of safety and protection. This merging of light represents a union, a deepening of your connection with Michael's essence.

As you continue to focus on this light, allow your mind to rest in stillness. Let go of any thoughts or expectations, surrendering fully to the experience. Trust that Michael's presence is guiding you, that his energy is working within you even if you cannot yet perceive it consciously. This meditation is a time for receptivity, a moment to simply be in his presence, to allow his energy to heal, protect, and uplift you.

You may begin to feel subtle shifts within—perhaps a warmth in your chest, a sense of calm spreading through your body, or even a gentle tingling in your hands. These sensations are signs that Michael's energy is flowing into you, a physical manifestation of his spiritual presence. Allow these feelings to deepen, letting them bring you fully into the present moment, a space where only peace and clarity exist.

If you wish to receive guidance from Michael, place a question or intention softly in your mind, something you are seeking insight on. This question should come from the heart, a sincere inquiry that reflects your true needs or desires. Once you have formed the question, release it into the light within your heart, surrendering it to Michael's wisdom. Trust that an answer will come in the way and time that is right, whether as a thought, an impression, a feeling, or even a realization that arises later. Michael's guidance is subtle yet profound, and it often speaks through intuition and insight rather than direct words.

Continue to rest in this space of connection, allowing yourself to simply be with Michael's presence. If thoughts arise, let them pass like clouds across a clear sky, gently bringing your focus back to the blue light within your heart. This practice of returning to the light strengthens your connection, teaching your mind to align with Michael's energy rather than distractions or worries. Over time, this alignment becomes easier, a natural rhythm that brings you into harmony with Michael's peace and protection.

As you near the end of the meditation, take a few moments to offer gratitude to Michael for his presence. Thank him for the guidance, protection, and strength he has shared with you in this sacred time. Feel his light beginning to settle within your heart, a warm glow that will remain with you even after the meditation ends. This light is a gift, a part of Michael's energy that you carry forward, a source of courage and peace that lives within you.

Before opening your eyes, take a few deep breaths, grounding yourself back into the physical world. Wiggle your fingers and toes, feeling the sensation in your body, the solidity of the ground beneath you. When you are ready, gently open your eyes, bringing with you the peace and clarity of Michael's presence into your day.

Meditating with Michael's presence is a practice you can return to whenever you seek his guidance or wish to deepen your connection. This meditation allows you to integrate his energy into your daily life, a reminder that his protection and wisdom are always within reach. With each session, you strengthen this connection, building a relationship with Michael that supports your growth, empowers your spirit, and brings peace to your mind.

As you continue this practice, you may find that Michael's presence begins to appear more readily, both in meditation and in moments of daily life. His energy becomes a familiar and comforting force, a quiet assurance that surrounds you in times of need. This connection is not just a momentary experience but a bond, a partnership that supports and guides you on your path.

With each meditation, you deepen your alignment with Michael's essence, inviting his courage, protection, and wisdom to become an integral part of who you are. This is the gift of meditating with Michael's presence—a journey of discovery, healing, and transformation, a path that brings you ever closer to the divine light within and around you, a light that forever illuminates your path with the strength and love of Archangel Michael.

Chapter 13
Receiving Divine Guidance

Receiving divine guidance from Archangel Michael is a journey of attunement, a practice of learning to recognize and trust the subtle ways in which his wisdom reaches you. Michael's guidance is both protective and empowering, offering clarity when you face uncertainty and strength when you encounter challenges. To receive his guidance is to open yourself to a higher perspective, a vision that transcends the limitations of everyday life and aligns with your soul's true path.

This chapter explores practices that cultivate receptivity, exercises that enable you to attune to Michael's voice and presence, and ways to interpret the signs and messages he sends. Divine guidance does not always arrive as a spoken word or direct sign; more often, it is a quiet nudge, a feeling, or an image that arises in the mind. Michael's guidance is powerful yet subtle, reaching you in moments of stillness, in symbols that resonate deeply, or through an inner knowing that guides you to the truth.

To begin receiving Michael's guidance, first cultivate a space of openness and receptivity within yourself. Guidance flows most clearly to a quiet mind and an open heart. In the same way that light cannot enter a closed room, divine messages struggle to penetrate a mind preoccupied with worries and doubts. Start with a practice of stillness, a moment each day where you sit in silence, allowing your mind to quiet. This daily space of silence becomes a fertile ground where Michael's guidance can be sensed and received without interference.

Create a simple ritual to invite his guidance into your life. Begin by lighting a candle, perhaps blue or white, as these colors resonate with Michael's energy. As you light the candle, set a clear intention, such as, "Archangel Michael, I open myself to your guidance. May I receive your wisdom with clarity, trust, and an open heart." Visualize his light surrounding you, creating a space of peace and safety. This intention signals your readiness, a call that Michael's presence can respond to directly.

In moments when you seek his guidance on specific matters, approach Michael with sincerity and simplicity. Close your eyes, center your awareness, and form your question in your mind or speak it aloud. This question should come from the heart, a genuine inquiry that invites clarity and insight. For example, you might ask, "Archangel Michael, what steps should I take to align with my highest path?" or "How can I find the courage to overcome this challenge?" Once you have asked your question, release it, trusting that the answer will come in the right time and way.

Michael's guidance often arrives in subtle forms. One of the most common ways he communicates is through **intuition**—a sudden insight, a feeling of certainty, or a quiet, persistent thought that gently guides you in a particular direction. These impressions may seem small or easily overlooked, but they are powerful signals. Trust your intuition, knowing that it is often the voice of divine guidance. When you feel an inner nudge or hear a quiet whisper in your mind, pause and listen deeply. Allow your intuition to unfold, letting it reveal insights that are both clear and grounded in truth.

In addition to intuition, Michael's messages frequently appear through **symbols**. These symbols can manifest in your daily life, perhaps as recurring images, dreams, or even phrases that catch your attention. Feathers, particularly blue or white, are a common sign of Michael's presence and protection. If you find a feather in an unexpected place, take it as a gentle reminder that he is watching over you, guiding and protecting you.

Symbols may also appear in numbers, sounds, or objects that seem to stand out. Repeated sequences, like seeing the number "111" or "444," can be signs that Michael's guidance is near. Pay attention to these patterns, as they may carry messages or insights meant specifically for you. Each symbol has a meaning, a vibration that speaks directly to your subconscious, often bypassing the analytical mind. When a symbol appears, trust that it has purpose, that it is Michael's way of reaching you in a form that resonates with your spirit.

Dreams are another powerful medium through which Michael communicates. As you sleep, the barriers of the conscious mind soften, allowing his guidance to flow more freely. Before bed, set an intention to receive insights or guidance through your dreams. You might say, "Archangel Michael, I ask for your guidance tonight. Help me to understand the messages my soul needs to hear." Keep a journal by your bedside, and upon waking, write down any dreams, symbols, or emotions you recall. Over time, you may notice recurring themes or patterns that reveal Michael's messages to you, helping you to navigate your path with clarity and courage.

In addition to these personal symbols, Michael's guidance can also be sensed through **synchronicities**—meaningful coincidences that seem to defy chance. These synchronicities often arise at pivotal moments, aligning people, events, or opportunities that reflect Michael's influence. For example, you may find that a book falls open to a passage that answers a question you've been pondering, or you meet someone who offers exactly the wisdom or support you need. These events are not random; they are the universe's way of arranging circumstances to provide guidance and direction. By staying open and observant, you recognize Michael's hand at work, guiding you through the intricate tapestry of life.

Another effective way to deepen your connection to Michael's guidance is through **journaling**. Writing is a form of release, a way to create space for intuition to flow. Begin by setting aside time each day to write freely, allowing your thoughts and feelings to pour onto the page without judgment or censorship. As you write, focus on questions or areas where you seek Michael's guidance. You may find that insights begin to emerge naturally, as though Michael's voice is guiding your hand, helping you uncover answers that were waiting within you. This practice of journaling opens a channel, a space where Michael's wisdom can flow directly into your awareness.

Guided **meditation** is another powerful practice to connect with Michael's guidance. Visualize a blue light surrounding you, inviting Michael's presence to come closer. Once you feel his energy, ask your question or state your intention for guidance, then sit in silence, allowing any impressions, thoughts, or feelings to surface. Michael's answers may arrive as visions, words, or simply a deep sense of knowing. This form of meditation creates a bridge between you and Michael, a space where his wisdom can reach you without interference from the conscious mind.

Sometimes, the guidance you seek may not arrive immediately. In such cases, practice **patience and trust**. Michael's answers come at the right time and in the form that best serves your highest good. Remember that his guidance may not always align with your expectations; it may challenge you to step outside your comfort zone, to trust a path that feels unfamiliar. Be open to the unexpected, knowing that Michael's perspective is broader and wiser, that he sees the entire journey while you see only a part. This trust is essential, a surrender that allows his guidance to flow more freely.

If you feel unsure about the guidance you receive, ask for **confirmation**. Michael's energy is clear and consistent; he is not bound by time and will repeat messages as needed to ensure you understand. If a sign or symbol appears multiple times or if you feel a recurring nudge, take it as confirmation of Michael's message. By honoring this process, you build a relationship based on trust, a connection where Michael's guidance becomes an ongoing dialogue, a conversation that grows clearer with each interaction.

With time, you may find that Michael's guidance becomes woven into the fabric of your daily life. His presence can be felt in the small moments, the quiet insights, the choices you make that align with your highest good. This guidance is not a series of commands; it is a gentle support, a reminder of the wisdom and courage that lie within you. Michael's role is not to direct every action but to empower you to trust your path, to walk it with strength, knowing that his energy is always with you.

As you deepen this practice, you will become more attuned to Michael's presence, able to sense his guidance in even the smallest details. This is a process of opening, a willingness to see beyond the surface and trust in the invisible connections that shape your path. Michael's guidance invites you to live with awareness, to approach each day with a sense of purpose and alignment, a readiness to embrace the signs and messages that come your way.

In receiving Michael's guidance, you step into a relationship of profound support and love. His wisdom is a gift, a resource that illuminates your path and strengthens your spirit. With each sign, each symbol, each quiet whisper of intuition, Michael's presence becomes more vivid, a constant light that shines upon your journey. Embrace this guidance with an open heart, knowing that with Michael by your side, you are always guided, always protected, and forever aligned with your soul's highest truth.

Chapter 14
Building Your Energetic Self-Defense

Creating energetic self-defense with Archangel Michael is an empowering practice, an act of spiritual self-care that reinforces your personal boundaries and shields your energy from negativity. Michael, as the protector archangel, provides a powerful source of light and strength, one that you can draw upon to establish a defense against harmful energies, thoughts, and emotions. Working with him to build your energetic self-defense is more than an exercise in protection; it is a commitment to maintaining your peace, grounding, and emotional resilience in an often chaotic world.

Energetic self-defense involves recognizing and strengthening the boundaries of your own energy field, creating a clear separation between your energy and external influences. Just as we maintain the health of our physical bodies, it is essential to care for our energetic well-being. With Archangel Michael's support, you can learn to sense, establish, and maintain an energetic barrier that keeps out negativity while allowing positive, nourishing energy to flow freely. This practice ensures that your spirit remains vibrant and centered, safeguarded against influences that may drain or destabilize you.

The first step in building energetic self-defense is to cultivate **awareness** of your personal energy. Your energy field, or aura, extends beyond your physical body, radiating and interacting with the energies around you. Begin by finding a quiet space where you can sit comfortably and focus inward. Close your eyes, take a few deep breaths, and center yourself. With each breath, allow your mind to become still, tuning into the subtle sensations within and around you.

In your mind's eye, visualize a gentle light surrounding your body, representing your energy field. This light may appear as a soft glow that extends about an arm's length around you, a sphere that encompasses your entire being. Notice how this light feels—is it bright and steady, or does it seem faint or dispersed? Are there any areas that feel tense, dense, or vulnerable? These observations provide insights into the current state of your energy, helping you identify areas that may need reinforcement.

Once you are aware of your energy, it is time to call upon Michael's protection. Visualize him standing beside you, radiating a strong, blue light that fills the space around you. In your mind or aloud, say, "Archangel Michael, I call upon you to strengthen my energy field. Surround me with your protective light and shield me from all negativity." As you speak, feel his energy merging with yours, reinforcing your boundaries and filling you with strength.

A powerful technique to establish your energetic self-defense is the **Blue Shield of Protection**. Imagine Michael extending his hand, drawing a shield of radiant blue light around your body. This shield acts as a filter, allowing in only positive, loving energies while blocking any harmful influences. See this shield as a semi-permeable boundary, one that protects without isolating, one that keeps you grounded yet open to the support of the divine.

As you visualize this shield, imagine it becoming denser and more resilient, a layer of Michael's energy that surrounds and fortifies your aura. You may choose to visualize it as a glowing, semi-transparent bubble that moves with you, a boundary that adapts to your movements, reinforcing itself each time you call upon it. This Blue Shield can be called upon whenever you feel exposed, anxious, or in need of extra protection. With practice, it will become a natural part of your energy field, a constant, protective presence that accompanies you.

Another technique to enhance your energetic self-defense is the **Cloak of Invisibility**. This cloak does not make you invisible in the literal sense but rather obscures your energy from others who may attempt to intrude or drain it. Visualize Michael placing a soft, blue cloak around you, covering your entire body, from head to toe. This cloak blends with your energy, concealing your light from any negative or intrusive forces. Imagine yourself moving through the world with this cloak, shielded and protected, your energy intact and inaccessible to anyone with harmful intentions.

The **Sword of Light**, another of Michael's symbols, can also be used to cut any energetic cords that drain or bind you. Energetic cords are connections between yourself and others, and while some cords represent positive bonds, others can be unhealthy or draining. Visualize Michael's sword in your hand, its blade glowing with a blue-white flame. See yourself gently but firmly cutting through any cords that feel restrictive, heavy, or invasive. As you do this, send love and release to the other person involved, freeing both of you from any energetic dependence.

Once you have cut these cords, visualize Michael's blue light sealing the areas where the cords were attached, reinforcing your energy field. This process allows you to retain your energy while remaining compassionate and free from attachment. Regularly using the Sword of Light to clear and cut cords is a practice of emotional independence, a way to honor your boundaries while still offering kindness and support from a balanced place.

Grounding is another essential component of energetic self-defense, anchoring you firmly to the earth and strengthening your resilience. To ground yourself, imagine roots extending from the base of your spine or the soles of your feet, reaching deep into the earth. As these roots grow, feel them connecting with the core of the earth, drawing up a stable, grounding energy that rises through your body. This energy fills your entire being, aligning and centering you, connecting you with the stability of the earth below and Michael's protective light above.

In situations that feel energetically challenging, use **affirmations** as another layer of defense. Affirmations are positive statements that reinforce your energetic boundaries and strengthen your self-worth. Examples include "I am surrounded by divine light and protection," "Only love and light may enter my space," or "I am safe, grounded, and at peace." Speak these affirmations with conviction, letting each word resonate within your energy field, strengthening your self-confidence and inner resolve. These affirmations are not just words; they are declarations of your sovereignty, a reminder that you are in control of your own energy.

Incorporate **crystals** as tools for energetic defense, as they hold grounding and protective properties that amplify Michael's energy. Stones like black tourmaline, obsidian, and hematite are known for their ability to absorb and deflect negativity, making them powerful allies in maintaining a strong energy field. Carry a piece of one of these stones with you, or place it near your workspace or home, using it as a touchstone that reminds you of Michael's protection. Holding or wearing these stones during meditation can also enhance your visualization practices, strengthening your energetic shield with their grounding energy.

In addition to these techniques, regular **spiritual cleansing** is essential for maintaining a protected and vibrant energy field. Use tools like sage, palo santo, or salt baths to cleanse your aura and clear away any negativity you may have absorbed. Imagine Michael's blue light sweeping through your energy field as you perform these cleansing rituals, purifying your spirit and restoring balance. Cleansing allows your energetic defenses to remain resilient, preventing the buildup of external energies that can weaken your boundaries over time.

One of the most profound aspects of building energetic self-defense is learning to trust your **intuition**. Your intuition serves as an early warning system, alerting you to situations or people that may be energetically draining or disruptive. When you sense discomfort or unease around certain individuals or environments, honor that feeling. Call upon Michael's protection, visualizing your Blue Shield or Cloak of Invisibility around you. Trusting your intuition is a key part of this practice, reinforcing the boundaries that keep your energy safe and allowing Michael's guidance to direct you away from potential harm.

As you continue working with Michael to build your energetic self-defense, you may notice a greater sense of confidence and peace in your daily life. This practice is not about creating walls but about fostering resilience, enabling you to interact with the world from a place of strength and security. With Michael's guidance, your energy field becomes both a sanctuary and a shield, a space where you are empowered, grounded, and aligned with your true self.

This ongoing practice of energetic self-defense is a journey of self-awareness, one that deepens your connection with Michael while strengthening your inner boundaries. By integrating these techniques into your life, you honor your well-being, creating a foundation of protection that supports your spiritual growth. Through this connection, you develop a strong, fortified spirit that can navigate life's challenges with grace and composure.

Each time you call upon Michael's protection, each time you reinforce your energy field, you affirm your commitment to maintaining a balanced, protected space within yourself. Michael's presence is always with you, a constant source of strength, guiding you toward a life of peace, integrity, and empowerment. Embrace this path with confidence, knowing that with Michael's guidance, you are forever shielded, safe, and free to live in alignment with your highest truth.

Chapter 15
Emotional Healing with Michael's Support

Emotional healing with the support of Archangel Michael is a journey of profound transformation, a process that brings peace and clarity to the heart by releasing burdens, traumas, and fears that no longer serve. Michael's presence is one of strength and compassion, offering both the courage to face difficult emotions and the reassurance that you are not alone in this journey. With his guidance, emotional wounds that may have felt overwhelming or deeply hidden can be gently brought to light, examined, and transformed. Michael does not shield us from these experiences but provides the strength needed to confront and heal them, restoring balance and peace within.

To begin this journey of emotional healing, it's important to create a safe and intentional space where Michael's presence can be felt. This space can be a quiet room, a secluded area in nature, or even a small corner in your home dedicated to your healing practice. Light a candle or hold a piece of lapis lazuli or rose quartz, stones that resonate with healing and compassion. As you settle into this space, take a few deep breaths, allowing each exhalation to release any tension or resistance. This is a sacred time for you to connect with your inner self and invite Michael's healing light into your heart.

When you feel ready, begin by calling upon Michael. In your mind or aloud, say, "Archangel Michael, I invite your presence into this space. Surround me with your strength and compassion as I open my heart to healing. Help me to release what no longer serves me, to find peace, and to rediscover my inner light." As you speak these words, visualize Michael appearing before you, a radiant figure surrounded by a blue aura of healing and protection. His energy is calm yet powerful, a presence that inspires trust and safety.

With Michael's presence beside you, take a moment to identify any emotions or memories that are weighing on your heart. These may be recent experiences or older wounds that have lingered over time. Allow these emotions to surface without judgment, observing them as they are, without the need to analyze or explain. Perhaps there is sadness, fear, anger, or regret—whatever arises, hold it gently in your awareness, knowing that it is safe to feel these emotions in Michael's presence.

One of the most powerful techniques for emotional healing with Michael is the **Release of the Blue Flame**. Visualize a brilliant blue flame in front of you, glowing with Michael's energy. This flame is not a destructive force but a purifying one, capable of transmuting heavy emotions into light. As you focus on this flame, imagine yourself placing each difficult emotion, memory, or fear into its gentle warmth. See the flame enveloping these energies, dissolving their weight, transforming them into pure light.

As you release each emotion into the flame, speak words of intention, such as, "I release this sadness to the light of healing," or "I surrender this fear to Michael's protection." With each statement, feel the emotion lifting from your heart, its weight gradually lessening as the flame works to cleanse and purify. This is a process of letting go, of trusting that Michael's energy can transform what feels painful into a source of strength and resilience.

During this process, you may feel sensations of warmth, tingling, or a lightness in your chest, signs that Michael's healing energy is working within you. These sensations are subtle yet profound, an indication that the release is taking place on an energetic level. Allow yourself to remain in this space of release for as long as you need, giving each emotion or memory the attention it requires before surrendering it fully.

For deeper emotional wounds, it can be helpful to work with **Michael's Sword of Light** to cut any lingering energetic cords connected to painful experiences or relationships. Emotional wounds often leave energetic imprints, attachments that tie us to past events and drain our vitality. Visualize Michael standing beside you, holding his sword, its blade glowing with a pure blue-white light. See him gently guiding the sword toward any cords or attachments that no longer serve you, his intention one of compassion and release.

As Michael's sword touches these cords, imagine them dissolving instantly, releasing you from any energetic binds. With each cut, feel a newfound freedom, a sense of independence from the weight of the past. This practice is not about forgetting but about releasing the emotional charge these experiences carry, allowing you to move forward without being bound by old wounds. With Michael's help, these attachments transform, freeing you to experience your life with renewed clarity and peace.

After working with the Blue Flame and the Sword of Light, you may wish to **place a hand over your heart** and take a few deep breaths, inviting compassion and gentleness toward yourself. Emotional healing is a delicate process, one that requires patience and self-acceptance. In this moment, imagine Michael placing his hand over yours, his energy flowing into your heart, filling you with warmth and reassurance. Feel his light soothing any areas of hurt or vulnerability, a balm that brings comfort and healing.

Michael's energy encourages you to be compassionate with yourself, to recognize that healing is not an instant process but a journey. Allow yourself to feel whatever emotions arise without judgment. If tears come, let them flow; if anger or frustration surfaces, acknowledge these feelings with kindness. Michael's presence provides a safe container for all emotions, a space where nothing is rejected or judged. Each emotion is a part of your healing, a step toward wholeness and inner peace.

To further support your emotional healing, practice **affirmations** that align with Michael's energy. Affirmations such as "I am worthy of healing and peace," "I release the past with love," and "I am supported and protected" help to reframe your inner dialogue, replacing fear or doubt with trust and self-compassion. Speak these affirmations in Michael's presence, feeling each word resonate within your heart. These affirmations are not merely statements; they are declarations of your readiness to embrace healing, a way of anchoring Michael's support within your being.

Another helpful practice is **journaling**, a way to express and process emotions that may feel complex or difficult to articulate. In Michael's presence, write freely about what you are experiencing, letting the words flow without editing or judgment. This process of writing allows you to release thoughts and feelings in a tangible way, helping you gain clarity and perspective. You may wish to address Michael directly in your writing, asking for his guidance, expressing your intentions for healing, or reflecting on insights that arise during your journaling.

If emotional healing feels overwhelming, use **guided visualization** to deepen your connection with Michael's comforting energy. Visualize yourself in a safe, peaceful place—a serene meadow, a quiet beach, or a forest bathed in sunlight. Imagine Michael sitting beside you, his presence steady and calm. In this visualization, speak with him openly, sharing your fears, your hopes, or your pain. Feel his compassion surrounding you, a reassurance that your feelings are seen, acknowledged, and honored. This visualization creates a sanctuary of healing, a place you can return to whenever you need Michael's comfort and support.

For those times when emotional wounds resurface unexpectedly, establish a **daily ritual of protection and grounding** to maintain your balance. Begin each morning by visualizing Michael's Blue Shield surrounding you, protecting you from energies that may trigger or amplify emotional pain. Take a few moments to ground yourself by imagining roots extending from your feet into the earth, drawing strength and stability into your body. This practice creates a foundation of resilience, empowering you to face emotional challenges with courage and calm.

With each healing session, you deepen your connection to Michael's transformative energy, building a relationship that supports your emotional well-being. His presence becomes a source of inner strength, a reminder that no emotion is too heavy, no wound too deep to be healed. Through his guidance, you learn to navigate your emotions with honesty and compassion, allowing yourself to feel without fear, to heal without judgment.

Emotional healing with Michael is not a destination but a continuous process, one that grows and evolves with you. As you release old patterns and embrace your true self, you create space for joy, peace, and self-love. This journey transforms not only your relationship with the past but also your outlook on the present and the future. Michael's energy is woven into every step, a constant reminder that you are safe, supported, and guided toward wholeness.

Each time you call upon Michael for emotional healing, you renew your commitment to your well-being, honoring the light within you. His presence empowers you to confront and release what no longer serves, allowing you to move forward unburdened and at peace. With Michael's support, you are free to live fully, to embrace your true self, and to experience life with a heart that is open, healed, and resilient.

Chapter 16
Restoring Physical Health

Archangel Michael's presence extends beyond spiritual guidance and protection; he also offers his healing energy to support the restoration of physical health. While traditionally known as a protector and guardian, Michael's energy carries a potent force of renewal that can strengthen, energize, and align the body with wellness. Physical healing with Michael is not just about alleviating symptoms but about harmonizing the body, mind, and spirit, bringing them into alignment to support lasting health. Working with Michael's energy opens a pathway to rejuvenation, encouraging the body to release stress, toxins, and imbalance, and allowing divine light to flow through every cell.

The journey of physical healing begins with the intention to invite Michael's healing energy into your body. This intention is the cornerstone of the healing process, as it creates an opening for his light to enter and flow through areas of discomfort or illness. Begin by finding a comfortable, quiet space where you can relax without interruptions. If you wish, light a blue candle as a symbol of Michael's presence or place a crystal, such as clear quartz or selenite, nearby to anchor his healing energy.

Settle into this space with a few deep breaths, allowing each exhalation to release tension from your body. As you breathe, feel yourself becoming calm and receptive, open to receiving Michael's energy. In your mind or aloud, say, "Archangel Michael, I invite your healing light into my body. Surround me with your strength, restore my health, and fill every cell with your protective and healing energy." As you speak, visualize a soft, blue light descending around you, enveloping you in a gentle cocoon of warmth and peace.

As Michael's light surrounds you, focus on the area of your body that needs healing. Whether it is a physical injury, chronic pain, or an area of tension, visualize this part of your body bathed in Michael's blue light. Imagine the light gently penetrating the cells, filling them with a soothing, revitalizing energy that dissolves pain, inflammation, or discomfort. See this blue light as a cleansing wave, washing through each cell, removing any stagnant or blocked energy, and restoring each cell to a state of balance and health.

To deepen this process, use **breathwork** to guide Michael's energy through your body. As you inhale, visualize the blue light entering the area of discomfort, and as you exhale, imagine releasing any pain, tension, or illness, allowing it to dissolve into the light. This rhythmic breathing serves as a channel for Michael's energy, helping it to flow smoothly and deeply into the areas that require healing. With each breath, feel his light moving deeper into the cells, restoring vitality and harmony.

If you experience chronic conditions or a general sense of fatigue, visualize Michael's blue light flowing through your entire body, not just one area. Imagine this light as a gentle waterfall, pouring down from above and filling you from head to toe. See the light cascading through each part of your body, cleansing and revitalizing every organ, muscle, and cell. As this light moves through you, feel it carrying away toxins, fatigue, and any form of imbalance, leaving your body refreshed and energized.

In addition to visualization, you can also use **affirmations** to anchor Michael's healing energy in your body. Affirmations such as "My body is filled with divine healing light," "Every cell is renewed and restored," and "I am supported by Michael's strength and protection" reinforce the healing process, aligning your mind and spirit with the intention of wellness. Speak these affirmations aloud or silently as you continue to visualize Michael's light moving through your body. Allow each affirmation to resonate deeply, transforming not only your physical body but also your beliefs about your capacity for healing.

Michael's **Sword of Light** can also play a role in physical healing, especially in releasing energetic attachments that may contribute to illness or fatigue. Sometimes, physical ailments are linked to lingering energetic cords or attachments that drain your vitality. Visualize Michael standing beside you, holding his sword with a blade that glows with a vibrant blue-white light. With his guidance, allow him to cut away any cords or attachments that no longer serve your highest good, releasing you from these energetic ties. As the cords dissolve, feel a surge of freedom, a lightness that permeates your entire being, clearing away anything that obstructs your body's natural state of wellness.

If you struggle with stress or anxiety, which often manifests physically, consider **grounding techniques** to strengthen your body's connection to the earth. Michael's energy is powerful yet grounding, capable of anchoring you in the present moment and relieving the physical effects of stress. Imagine roots growing from your feet, extending deep into the earth, connecting you to its steady, nurturing energy. Feel Michael's presence guiding these roots, ensuring that you are firmly grounded and supported. This grounding practice can reduce physical tension, bringing calm to your muscles and organs, creating a foundation for healing to take place.

For specific injuries or areas of intense pain, use **focused visualization** with Michael's healing energy. Place your hand over the area, or simply hold your awareness there, and visualize a beam of blue light flowing from Michael directly into this spot. See this light pulsating gently, its energy entering the tissues, relieving pain, and accelerating healing. If you feel guided, imagine Michael placing his hand over yours, his energy flowing through you, amplifying your intention and infusing the area with a potent force of healing and renewal.

Journaling can also serve as a supportive practice for physical healing, as it allows you to explore any emotional patterns or thoughts that may be affecting your body. Physical health is often intertwined with emotional well-being, and by bringing awareness to unresolved emotions, you create space for healing on all levels. Write about your physical sensations, any pain or discomfort, and allow your thoughts to flow freely onto the page. As you write, invite Michael's guidance, asking him to reveal any insights or connections between your emotions and physical symptoms. This process can uncover valuable insights, helping you address not only the symptoms but the deeper causes of physical imbalance.

If you are working with specific health conditions, consider asking Michael to **guide you toward supportive resources**—whether doctors, treatments, or natural remedies that align with your path to wellness. His guidance often arrives in subtle ways, perhaps through an unexpected recommendation, a conversation, or a strong feeling of resonance with a particular approach. By opening yourself to his guidance, you can trust that you will be led to the resources and support systems that best serve your healing journey.

Another way to enhance physical healing is to integrate **meditation and relaxation techniques** that allow Michael's energy to work within your body without resistance. Stress and tension can create barriers that obstruct the flow of healing energy. Daily meditation, especially with Michael's presence, brings relaxation to the body, allowing it to enter a state of rest where healing can occur naturally. As you meditate, imagine Michael's blue light surrounding you, easing tension from each muscle, bringing peace to your mind, and fostering an environment where the body's natural healing processes are activated.

For chronic health challenges, establishing a **daily healing routine** with Michael can be particularly beneficial. This routine can be as simple as a few minutes each morning and evening spent visualizing his light within your body, speaking affirmations, or practicing gentle breathwork. This daily practice creates a consistent flow of healing energy, reinforcing your body's natural strength and resilience. Each day, you become more attuned to Michael's presence, allowing his light to support you as you move through the phases of your healing journey.

Remember, physical healing is a process that unfolds at its own pace, and patience with yourself is essential. Michael's support is a constant, reassuring presence, a reminder that healing is not only possible but part of your journey toward wholeness. When setbacks occur, or if the healing process feels slow, trust that each moment is bringing you closer to health, that Michael's light continues to work within you, even when the progress feels subtle or unseen.

To close each healing session, offer gratitude to Michael, acknowledging his presence and the light he has brought into your body. In your mind or aloud, say, "Thank you, Archangel Michael, for your healing light, for your protection, and for your strength. May I continue to grow in health and wholeness, aligned with your divine guidance." As you speak these words, visualize his light gently settling within you, a lasting energy that supports your body's ongoing restoration.

With each healing session, with each moment of connection to Michael's energy, you are building a foundation of strength, resilience, and well-being. His presence becomes an integral part of your journey, a source of protection and renewal that empowers you to face challenges with courage and hope. Physical healing with Michael is not only about the restoration of the body but about embracing a path of harmony, a journey that aligns your physical health with your spiritual growth.

As you continue this practice, you will find that Michael's energy becomes a constant support, a light that you can call upon whenever you need healing, strength, or reassurance. His guidance leads you toward wellness, his light fills you with peace, and his presence reminds you that you are never alone. Through his support, you are empowered to live fully, with a body that is healed, a spirit that is strong, and a heart that is open to the fullness of life.

Chapter 17
Purifying Environments with Michael

Creating a purified environment is essential for maintaining a space where harmony, clarity, and positive energy can flourish. Our surroundings deeply influence our well-being, and just as we cleanse our own energy, it is equally vital to cleanse the spaces we occupy. By working with Archangel Michael, we invite his potent, protective energy into our environment, removing negativity and replacing it with light and peace. Michael's presence acts as a powerful purifier, sweeping through spaces and transforming them into sanctuaries where our minds can rest, our spirits can expand, and our hearts can find peace.

When purifying your environment with Michael's assistance, you establish a space that is not only free from unwanted energies but is also fortified against negativity. This process creates a foundation of stability, a physical setting that supports your spiritual growth and well-being. Michael's purifying energy removes residual vibrations from past events, emotions, or conflicts that may have left an imprint, allowing the space to feel fresh, revitalized, and protected. Each time you cleanse a space with his energy, you make it a sacred place, a site of divine peace and strength.

To begin, choose the space you wish to purify—whether it is your home, a single room, or even your workspace. Gather any items you may wish to incorporate, such as a blue candle to represent Michael's presence, crystals like black tourmaline or selenite for added cleansing power, and a smudging tool such as sage, palo santo, or incense. These items are not essential but can act as physical aids, anchoring Michael's energy in the space. Arrange them thoughtfully, setting the intention that they are there to assist you in calling upon Michael's energy for purification.

As you prepare, take a few moments to center yourself. Close your eyes and take several deep breaths, allowing each exhale to release any distractions, bringing your awareness fully into the present moment. In your mind or aloud, say, "Archangel Michael, I invite you to join me in this space. Surround me with your purifying light and help me cleanse this environment. May it be filled with peace, clarity, and protection." As you speak, visualize Michael appearing beside you, his figure radiant with blue light, a presence that brings calm, strength, and reassurance.

To initiate the purification, begin at the entrance of the room or home. Light your smudging tool or candle, and as the smoke or light fills the air, visualize it carrying away any stagnant or negative energy. Move through the space slowly, guiding the smoke or candlelight along walls, in corners, and in places where energy may feel heavy. As you do this, imagine Michael walking beside you, his blue light expanding to every corner, purifying the space. Feel his energy sweeping through, a gentle yet powerful force that lifts away anything that does not serve your highest good.

As you move through each area, speak words of intention, such as, "I cleanse this space of all negativity," or "Only love and peace may dwell here." Let your words be a declaration, an affirmation that this space is sacred and protected. Michael's presence amplifies these intentions, sealing each area with his light, transforming it into a sanctuary of peace. This practice is especially beneficial in spaces that feel particularly dense or have experienced conflict, as it invites Michael's energy to reset and renew the atmosphere.

In areas where energy feels especially heavy, you may choose to visualize Michael's **Sword of Light** sweeping through, cutting through any dense or lingering vibrations. See him raising his sword, its blade glowing with a brilliant blue-white light, and slicing through the energy, dissolving it instantly into light. This visualization is particularly effective for spaces that feel resistant to purification or that seem to hold onto past energies. The Sword of Light acts as a catalyst, breaking up these denser energies and clearing the way for fresh, positive vibrations to enter.

Once you have moved through the entire space, return to the center of the room or home, and stand still, allowing Michael's energy to settle. Close your eyes and visualize a **blue flame** in the center of the space, a flame that represents his presence, a beacon of purity and protection. Imagine this flame expanding slowly, filling the entire room with a warm, blue light. See this light moving through every wall, every corner, every object, infusing each one with a purifying energy that dissolves any remaining negativity. This flame becomes a permanent symbol of Michael's guardianship, a reminder that his protection and peace permeate the space.

Next, visualize a **Blue Shield** surrounding the space. This shield acts as a protective barrier, preventing negative energies from entering. See Michael raising his hand, extending his energy to create a bubble or dome of blue light around your space. This shield is strong yet gentle, a boundary that allows positive energy to flow freely while blocking out any harmful or disruptive forces. Imagine this shield as semi-transparent, radiating a soft blue glow that reflects Michael's presence. This Blue Shield remains even after the ritual, a lasting layer of protection that guards your space against negativity.

To complete the ritual, take a moment to offer gratitude to Michael for his assistance. In your mind or aloud, say, "Thank you, Archangel Michael, for your guidance, protection, and cleansing light. May this space remain a sanctuary of peace, love, and strength, forever aligned with your divine presence." As you speak these words, imagine Michael's figure gently dissolving, his light remaining in the space as a constant presence, a source of purity and peace.

For added support, you may wish to place **protective crystals** around the room or home, particularly in entryways or windows, where energy enters. Stones like black tourmaline, obsidian, and amethyst are excellent choices, as they absorb and deflect negative energy. As you place each stone, visualize Michael's light flowing into it, empowering it to serve as an extension of his protection. These stones act as energetic filters, continuously working to keep your space clear and balanced.

Incorporating **salt** can also enhance the cleansing process, as salt has natural purifying properties. Sprinkle a small amount of salt in each corner of the room or across thresholds, setting the intention that the salt absorbs any remaining negativity. Afterward, vacuum or sweep it up, visualizing any unwanted energy being removed with it. This simple act reinforces Michael's energy within the space, anchoring his presence and ensuring that only positive vibrations remain.

If you experience frequent negativity in your space or feel that energy accumulates quickly, consider establishing a **regular purification practice** with Michael. You may choose to repeat this cleansing ritual weekly or monthly, depending on your needs. Consistent purification ensures that your environment remains aligned with Michael's energy, a space where peace and clarity can thrive. Each time you call upon him, you reinforce the protection he offers, building an atmosphere of unwavering positivity and light.

For those moments when you need a quick cleansing, visualize **Michael's Blue Flame** igniting instantly in the center of the room. See this flame expanding outward, purifying the space within seconds, refreshing the energy and restoring balance. This quick visualization can be done anytime, even in public spaces or when traveling, to instantly cleanse and fortify the area with Michael's presence.

When you purify your environment with Michael's assistance, you transform it into a place of rest, healing, and inspiration. His energy becomes a part of the space itself, a silent guardian that protects, uplifts, and renews. Each time you enter this purified environment, you feel his presence around you, a reminder that you are held in his light, shielded from negativity, and free to live and grow in a space that resonates with peace.

Over time, as you continue this practice, you may notice a lasting shift in the energy of your environment. Spaces that once felt dense or uncomfortable will transform, becoming places where you feel refreshed, inspired, and supported. Michael's presence grows stronger with each purification, creating a sanctuary where you can connect with yourself, with him, and with the divine. Through this sacred space, you cultivate an atmosphere that nurtures your highest self, a place of beauty, calm, and spiritual alignment.

By inviting Michael's energy into your environment, you create a foundation of light that supports you in every aspect of your life. This purified space becomes a reflection of your inner peace, a mirror of the clarity, protection, and strength that Michael brings to your journey. As you walk this path, know that with Michael's guidance, your surroundings are forever protected, forever filled with his unwavering light and love.

Chapter 18
Daily Spiritual Protection

Daily spiritual protection with Archangel Michael is a practice that strengthens and shields the soul, helping you move through each day with confidence, peace, and resilience. By engaging with Michael's protective energy every day, you create a shield around yourself that guards against negative influences, environmental stressors, and unwanted energies. This daily practice is not only an act of self-care but a reaffirmation of your commitment to living in alignment with your highest self, fortified by Michael's enduring presence.

Working with Michael on a daily basis transforms protection from a single act into a steady foundation, a constant support that surrounds you as you navigate life. It creates a shield that can be strengthened whenever needed, a spiritual armor that reflects Michael's qualities of courage, strength, and compassion. This daily ritual becomes a touchstone, a practice that invites Michael's guidance and establishes a deep-rooted connection with his energy, ensuring that his light accompanies you wherever you go.

Begin your daily protection practice in the morning, ideally as soon as you wake. By starting your day with this ritual, you establish a foundation of peace and resilience that supports you through every encounter, interaction, and experience. Find a quiet space where you can focus without distraction, even if only for a few moments. Sit comfortably, close your eyes, and take several deep breaths. As you inhale, feel yourself drawing in

Michael's energy; as you exhale, release any tension, worry, or fatigue from the night before.

With your mind centered and your breath steady, call upon Michael's presence. In your mind or aloud, say, "Archangel Michael, I invite you into my day. Surround me with your protective light, guide me with your strength, and shield me from all harm. May I carry your courage and peace with me wherever I go." As you speak, visualize Michael standing before you, radiating a powerful blue light that begins to expand, enveloping your entire being.

Imagine this blue light forming a protective shield around you, a vibrant yet gentle barrier that moves with you, flexible yet impenetrable. This shield becomes a boundary that filters out any negativity, allowing only love, peace, and positivity to enter. Visualize the light growing brighter, reinforcing itself with each breath, forming a cocoon that guards your energy from external disturbances. This is Michael's Blue Shield, a layer of spiritual protection that stays with you throughout the day.

To deepen the strength of this shield, imagine **Michael's Sword of Light** hovering above you, its blade glowing with a blue-white flame. Visualize Michael lowering this sword over you, tracing it along the edge of the shield. As the sword moves, it seals the shield with an unbreakable strength, a layer of Michael's energy that protects against any negative or harmful forces. This act is both symbolic and energetic, a way of anchoring Michael's protective presence within your daily aura.

Once the shield is established, turn your attention inward, focusing on your heart. Visualize a small flame of blue light within your heart center, a spark of Michael's energy that will guide and protect you throughout the day. This flame represents not only his protection but his courage and wisdom. As you go about your day, this inner flame serves as a reminder of Michael's presence, a constant source of strength that you can return to whenever needed. Each time you feel unsure or vulnerable, visualize this flame brightening, filling you with a renewed sense of security and clarity.

Another powerful daily tool for spiritual protection is the **Cloak of Invisibility**. This cloak serves as a barrier that shields your energy from those who might seek to drain or intrude upon it. Visualize Michael placing this cloak around your shoulders, a soft, flowing garment of blue light that merges with your aura, making you energetically invisible to any forces that do not align with love and peace. The Cloak of Invisibility allows you to move through the day protected and unnoticed by negative influences, an energy boundary that keeps you grounded and safe.

Throughout the day, incorporate brief moments of **breathwork** to reinforce Michael's protective energy. Whenever you feel tension, stress, or negativity beginning to creep in, pause for a moment, take a deep breath, and imagine Michael's blue light filling your lungs and expanding outward. With each exhale, release any stress or unease, sending it into the earth to be purified. This simple breathwork practice creates a reset, allowing Michael's energy to clear away any disruptions and realign you with your inner peace.

In addition to these visualizations, **affirmations** are a valuable tool for strengthening spiritual protection. Begin each morning by reciting a few affirmations that align with Michael's qualities, such as, "I am protected by Archangel Michael's light," "Only love and peace may enter my space," or "I walk with courage, guided and guarded by Michael's presence." Let each word resonate within you, reinforcing your intention to remain connected to Michael's protective energy throughout the day.

When you encounter environments or interactions that feel particularly challenging, use **grounding techniques** to keep your energy stable and secure. Visualize roots extending from the base of your spine or feet, reaching deep into the earth. Feel the strength of the earth beneath you, supporting and grounding you. Imagine Michael's energy anchoring you to this grounding, ensuring that you remain centered and calm, no matter what energies surround you. Grounding in Michael's presence creates a solid foundation, allowing his energy to support you even in the most chaotic situations.

As your day progresses, stay aware of your energy, checking in periodically to assess how your protective shield feels. If you notice any weakening of the shield or sense any negativity entering your space, visualize Michael's Blue Shield once more, allowing it to brighten and strengthen. Imagine Michael standing beside you, reinforcing the shield with his light, restoring its power. This visualization takes only a few moments but can be a powerful reset, keeping you aligned with his protection.

At the end of each day, as part of your evening ritual, take a few moments to cleanse your energy and release any lingering influences. Begin by visualizing a **Blue Flame** in front of you, a flame of Michael's energy that burns away any negativity you may have picked up throughout the day. Imagine yourself stepping into this flame, feeling it envelop you completely, purifying your aura and restoring your energy to a state of peace. This is a time to release any stress, anxiety, or unwanted emotions, allowing Michael's light to clear your energy field.

As you step out of the flame, take a few deep breaths, feeling light and refreshed. Visualize your inner flame in your heart once more, a steady glow that will remain with you even as you sleep, a silent guardian of peace and strength. Thank Michael for his guidance, protection, and light throughout the day. This gratitude closes the ritual, honoring his presence and reaffirming your connection to his energy.

For additional support, consider keeping **protective crystals** nearby, such as black tourmaline, amethyst, or hematite. Carry these stones with you during the day, or place them near your bed at night. These crystals act as anchors for Michael's energy, reinforcing your shield and absorbing any negative energies. Hold them in your hand whenever you need a moment of protection or grounding, letting their energy merge with Michael's presence to strengthen your spiritual armor.

Finally, consider using **prayers or invocations** as daily anchors for Michael's protection. Simple phrases such as, "Archangel Michael, surround me with your light and protect me in all ways," can be repeated whenever you need reassurance or strength. These prayers create a direct connection to Michael, a call for his guidance and protection that can be invoked at any moment. By keeping these prayers close to your heart, you establish a steady, reliable line to his energy, reinforcing your spiritual protection throughout each day.

Over time, this daily protection practice becomes second nature, a seamless part of your life. The shield you create with Michael grows stronger with each day, a resilient boundary that safeguards your energy and peace of mind. Michael's presence becomes woven into your everyday routine, a steady light that accompanies you in all things. This practice is not only a form of protection but a foundation of empowerment, a reminder that you walk each day guided and guarded by a divine force.

Through this daily practice, you build a life where you feel safe, supported, and at peace, regardless of external circumstances. With Michael's energy by your side, you are free to move through life with courage, clarity, and confidence. His light serves as a reminder that you are forever protected, forever loved, and forever aligned with a higher power that watches over you.

Each morning, each breath, each moment you call upon Michael's protection is an affirmation of your strength, a dedication to live fully and freely in his light. With Michael's presence beside you, you are shielded from harm, empowered to face any challenge, and blessed with a peace that endures, grounded in the infinite love and wisdom of Archangel Michael.

Chapter 19
Overcoming Fears with Michael's Help

Overcoming fear with Archangel Michael's guidance is an invitation to step into courage and strength, allowing his presence to dissolve the anxieties and limitations that hold you back. Fear is a powerful emotion, often rooted in past experiences or shaped by uncertainties about the future. Michael's energy offers a profound pathway to freedom from fear, replacing it with a sense of peace, resilience, and confidence. Working with him in this way is about transforming fear into an opportunity for growth, enabling you to embrace life with a spirit of trust and faith.

Michael's support in overcoming fear is a reminder that fear itself is not a barrier but a signal, a call to explore and understand parts of ourselves that may feel vulnerable. Through his guidance, you learn to see fear not as an obstacle but as a gateway—a place where the soul is invited to expand and discover its true strength. Michael's role as protector makes him uniquely suited to help you release fears that may be hidden deep within, bringing his unwavering light into the places where shadows once lingered.

To begin your work with Michael on releasing fear, find a comfortable, quiet space where you can focus without distraction. Start by closing your eyes, taking several deep breaths, and allowing your body to relax. With each exhale, imagine releasing any tension, worries, or anxieties, letting them drift away like clouds dissolving in the sky. In this relaxed state, invite Michael to join you, asking for his support and protection. In your mind or aloud, say, "Archangel Michael, I ask for your presence to help me release my fears. Surround me with your light and guide me into a place of peace and courage."

As you call upon Michael, visualize him appearing before you, radiating a strong, comforting blue light. Feel his presence surrounding you, a shield that keeps you safe and steady as you face the journey ahead. His energy brings a sense of calm and reassurance, allowing you to open up to any emotions or fears that arise without feeling overwhelmed. Take a moment to rest in this light, letting it fill your heart and mind with peace, grounding you in Michael's strength and protection.

One powerful technique for releasing fear is to use **visualization** to transform it. Begin by identifying a specific fear or worry that you wish to release. This might be a fear of failure, a fear of judgment, or a fear rooted in past experiences. Bring this fear into your awareness, allowing yourself to acknowledge it without judgment. Visualize this fear as a tangible object—a stone, a piece of dark mist, or any image that feels true to you. The goal is to give form to the fear so that you can work with it directly.

Now, imagine placing this fear into a **Blue Flame** that stands before you, a flame created by Michael's energy. See the fear dissolving as it touches the flame, the blue light gently consuming it, transforming its dark energy into light. As the fear dissolves, feel a weight lifting from you, a sense of release that brings new clarity and peace. With each breath, imagine more of this fear dissolving, until the flame has fully transmuted it into light. This visualization is not merely symbolic; it is an energetic act, a way of releasing the hold that fear has on you.

As the fear dissolves, imagine Michael placing his **Sword of Light** in your hands. This sword is a tool of courage and truth, a symbol that you are protected and empowered. Feel its energy merging with yours, a reminder that you have the strength to face anything. Visualize yourself holding the sword high, its blade glowing with a pure blue light that represents Michael's courage. In this moment, affirm your willingness to face life without fear. Say, "I release my fears and embrace the strength within me.

With Michael's support, I am free to live in courage, guided by truth and light."

Another effective method is to work with **affirmations** that resonate with Michael's energy of strength and protection. These affirmations serve as reminders of your inner resilience and the divine support that is always available. Examples include: "I am safe, supported, and fearless," "I trust in Michael's protection as I release all fear," or "Courage flows through me as I walk my path." Speak these affirmations aloud, letting each word resonate deeply within you. With each repetition, you reinforce your intention to live beyond fear, inviting Michael's energy to fortify your spirit.

If you find that certain fears feel resistant or difficult to release, use **guided breathwork** to create space within. Begin by breathing deeply, focusing on the area of your body where the fear feels most present. This might be in your chest, stomach, or any place where tension gathers. Imagine breathing Michael's blue light into this area, filling it with warmth and peace. With each exhale, release some of the tension, allowing the fear to soften and dissolve. This breathwork practice allows Michael's energy to move into places that feel constricted, freeing the fear from within.

Michael can also assist in overcoming **fears rooted in past experiences or traumas**. These deep-seated fears may stem from specific events that left a lingering emotional imprint. To address these, visualize Michael standing beside you, his hand resting on your shoulder in support. Imagine him guiding you to revisit the memory, not to relive it but to see it through his eyes— a perspective filled with compassion and understanding. As you observe the memory, imagine Michael's light surrounding it, transforming any residual pain or fear into peace. Allow his energy to help you see this past event with a new perspective, one that frees you from its grip and restores your sense of inner peace.

If you encounter fears related to **the future or the unknown**, work with Michael's **Blue Shield** as a tool for trust and stability. Visualize this shield surrounding you, creating a boundary that keeps worries about the future from clouding your present. With this shield in place, feel a sense of confidence in each step forward, knowing that Michael's energy surrounds you and that you are guided at every moment. Each time you feel uncertain or fearful about the future, return to this visualization, grounding yourself in Michael's light, which serves as a constant reminder of divine protection.

For fears that arise suddenly or during the day, create a quick **mental check-in** with Michael. When fear surfaces, pause for a moment, close your eyes, and imagine Michael standing beside you, his hand on your shoulder. Feel his presence calming and steadying you, a reminder that you are safe. In this brief moment, acknowledge the fear without attaching to it, then release it into Michael's light. This practice allows you to return to a place of calm and clarity whenever fear arises, no matter where you are.

To strengthen your resilience over time, establish a **daily practice of courage** with Michael's guidance. Each morning, as part of your spiritual routine, call upon him to infuse you with strength and fortitude. Visualize his energy filling your heart, creating a wellspring of courage that you can draw upon throughout the day. This daily ritual serves as a foundation, fortifying your inner strength and making it easier to face challenges without allowing fear to take root.

Journaling is another powerful tool for understanding and releasing fears. Write openly about the fears you experience, describing them in detail and reflecting on any patterns you notice. Ask Michael for guidance in uncovering the deeper reasons behind these fears and allow your writing to flow freely. As insights emerge, notice any moments of clarity or understanding that arise. This journaling process helps you see your fears objectively, breaking them down into manageable pieces and making it easier to address them with Michael's support.

To complete each session of working with Michael on overcoming fear, take a moment to offer gratitude. In your mind or aloud, say, "Thank you, Archangel Michael, for guiding me through my fears, for illuminating the path of courage, and for standing by my side." Feel his light within you, a permanent source of strength that empowers you to walk forward with confidence and faith. This gratitude closes the session, reaffirming the bond you share with Michael and reinforcing your intention to live beyond fear.

Over time, as you continue this work with Michael, you may notice that fears that once seemed insurmountable lose their power over you. His presence brings a sense of freedom, a lightness that comes from knowing you are protected and supported. This process of overcoming fear is not about erasing it but about transforming it, learning to view each moment of uncertainty as a chance to deepen your connection with Michael's guidance and discover the courage within.

With Michael's support, you build a life where fear no longer holds you back but instead serves as a stepping stone toward growth. His energy reminds you that courage is not the absence of fear but the decision to move forward with faith. Through his presence, you are empowered to live boldly, to trust in the journey, and to face each day with a heart that is open, resilient, and fearless.

Chapter 20
Freeing Yourself from Harmful Habits

With Archangel Michael's guidance, the journey of releasing harmful habits becomes a path of liberation and transformation, a process that invites you to step fully into a life of health, clarity, and alignment with your highest self. Harmful habits, whether they manifest as behaviors, thought patterns, or dependencies, often serve as barriers that limit our growth and drain our energy. Michael's powerful and protective energy assists you in breaking these patterns, helping you to release attachments that no longer serve you and creating space for positive, life-affirming choices to take root.

This chapter explores how Michael's strength can be invoked to free yourself from these habits, replacing them with practices that support your spiritual, emotional, and physical well-being. His support is steadfast and unwavering, providing not only the courage to face these habits honestly but also the energy to transform and heal. In working with Michael, the process of overcoming harmful habits is not about judgment or punishment but about releasing what no longer serves and embracing the freedom that lies on the other side.

Begin by setting a clear and compassionate intention to release the habit you wish to overcome. This intention is crucial, as it serves as both a guide and an anchor during moments of challenge. Find a quiet space to sit comfortably, take a few deep breaths, and center yourself. Call upon Michael, inviting him to join you in this journey. In your mind or aloud, say, "Archangel Michael, I invite your presence and strength to help me release this habit. Surround me with your light, support me in my resolve, and help me find freedom and peace." As you speak, visualize Michael standing before you, his blue light enveloping you with a powerful, supportive energy.

One of the most effective ways to work with Michael on releasing harmful habits is through **visualization**. Begin by identifying the habit you wish to release. This habit could be anything that drains your energy, limits your potential, or disrupts your well-being, such as procrastination, excessive worry, self-criticism, or a dependency on substances or behaviors. Hold this habit in your mind, acknowledging its presence without judgment. Visualize it as an object or shape, something tangible that you can hold or see. This object may appear dark, heavy, or clouded, representing the energy of the habit.

Now, imagine placing this object into a **Blue Flame** that Michael has created before you. This flame glows with a vibrant, pure blue light, a light that has the power to cleanse and transform. See the habit dissolving as it touches the flame, breaking down into particles of light that float away, leaving only a sense of clarity and lightness behind. This visualization symbolizes the release of the habit's grip on you, a letting go of its energy and influence. With each breath, feel more of the habit dissolving, its hold on you loosening, until the flame has completely purified it.

To deepen this release, use **affirmations** to reinforce your intention. Affirmations create a new mental framework that supports your desire to move beyond the habit. Speak phrases such as, "I am free from this habit," "I am strong and capable of positive change," or "With Michael's support, I embrace my highest potential." Let each affirmation resonate deeply within you, replacing the old patterns with empowering beliefs. These affirmations are not simply words; they are declarations of your commitment to transformation, statements that invite Michael's energy to fortify your resolve.

For habits rooted in emotional triggers, consider working with **Michael's Sword of Light**. Emotional attachments often tie us to harmful habits, creating cycles that are difficult to break. Visualize Michael standing beside you, his sword glowing with a pure blue-white flame. In your mind, identify any emotional attachments or triggers that contribute to the habit, perhaps rooted in stress, past pain, or unresolved feelings. Imagine these attachments as cords connected to you, each one representing a link that holds you to the habit.

With compassion and clarity, see Michael's sword gently cutting each cord, releasing you from the emotional ties that bind you to the habit. As each cord dissolves, feel a weight lifting, a sense of freedom expanding within you. Michael's sword does not sever your emotions but rather liberates you from patterns that are no longer helpful. This practice allows you to acknowledge and honor your emotions without being bound by them, creating space for healthier responses and behaviors.

If you experience cravings or urges related to the habit, turn to **breathwork** as a way to refocus and ground yourself. When the urge arises, pause, close your eyes, and take a deep breath, visualizing Michael's blue light entering your body with each inhale. As you exhale, release the craving or urge into his light, imagining it dissolving completely. Continue this breathing until you feel a sense of calm and control returning. This breathwork creates a moment of mindfulness, breaking the automatic response to the craving and allowing Michael's energy to guide you back to a place of peace.

In moments of vulnerability or temptation, the **Blue Shield of Protection** can be a powerful ally. Visualize this shield surrounding you, a protective barrier that keeps unwanted energies and impulses at bay. This shield acts as a boundary, helping you maintain your focus and resolve. Imagine Michael reinforcing this shield with his light, making it resilient and unbreakable. Each time you visualize this shield, you are reminded of your strength and commitment, a visible sign of Michael's support that accompanies you wherever you go.

For habits that feel deeply ingrained, consider establishing a **daily routine of intention-setting** with Michael. Each morning, call upon him to help you stay strong and aligned with your goal. Begin the day by placing a hand over your heart, taking a deep breath, and saying, "Archangel Michael, I dedicate this day to freedom from [name of habit]. Walk with me, support me, and help me make choices that serve my highest self." This intention-setting ritual serves as a daily anchor, a practice that grounds you in your purpose and invites Michael's guidance throughout the day.

Writing can also be a powerful tool for understanding and releasing harmful habits. Begin a **journal dedicated to your journey** of transformation, using it to explore the roots of the habit, reflect on your progress, and track moments of growth. Ask Michael for insights, writing down any feelings, thoughts, or images that arise. This journal becomes a place of healing, a space where you can witness your journey without judgment and acknowledge each step forward, no matter how small.

If the habit has been a part of your life for a long time, approach it with **compassion and patience**. Habits often form over years, and breaking them is a gradual process. Michael's energy encourages self-kindness, a reminder that transformation is a journey, not an overnight event. In moments of frustration or self-criticism, call upon Michael's compassion, allowing his light to ease any feelings of guilt or disappointment. With each setback, Michael's presence offers a reminder that every effort, every small choice toward change, is a step toward freedom.

As you progress, celebrate each milestone, no matter how small. Acknowledge each day that you successfully align with your intention, allowing yourself to feel pride in the progress you are making. Michael's energy is not only one of protection but of empowerment, a force that lifts you up and encourages you to see the strength within. Every step forward is a testament to your commitment, a reflection of your willingness to embrace positive change.

To conclude each session of working with Michael on releasing harmful habits, take a moment to offer gratitude. In your mind or aloud, say, "Thank you, Archangel Michael, for your guidance, strength, and support. I honor this journey and embrace the freedom that awaits." Feel his light within you, a source of ongoing strength and reassurance. This gratitude closes the session, affirming your commitment and reinforcing your connection to his energy.

As you continue this journey with Michael, you may notice a gradual shift—a lightness, a clarity, and a sense of freedom that grows each day. His presence provides a foundation of courage, allowing you to release what no longer serves you and embrace a life aligned with your true self. With each step, you are reminded that you are supported, protected, and fully capable of transformation.

Overcoming harmful habits with Michael's guidance is a path of self-discovery, a process that reveals your inner resilience and commitment to growth. His energy empowers you to face each challenge with confidence, to trust in your capacity for change, and to walk forward with a heart that is open, free, and aligned with the highest truth. Through this journey, you not only release what holds you back but also discover the boundless potential within, a life empowered by choice, courage, and Michael's unwavering support.

Chapter 21
Manifesting Goals with Michael

Manifesting your goals with the guidance of Archangel Michael is an empowering process that blends spiritual alignment with practical intention, enabling you to bring your deepest desires and aspirations into reality. Michael's energy is one of strength, clarity, and divine purpose, qualities that make him an invaluable ally in the manifestation process. With his support, you learn to channel your intentions through a lens of integrity, transforming dreams into achievable, tangible outcomes. Through Michael's guidance, the journey of manifestation becomes not only a pursuit of personal goals but an act of alignment with your highest path.

Working with Michael to manifest your goals means infusing each intention with purpose, a commitment to serve both your highest self and the greater good. Michael's approach to manifestation encourages a balance of intention and action, teaching you to trust in the process while also taking practical steps toward your desires. This chapter will guide you through methods for calling upon Michael's energy to support your goals, helping you to manifest them with confidence, clarity, and resilience.

To begin, it is essential to identify your goals with clarity. Sit in a quiet space where you can reflect and tune into your inner desires. Take a few deep breaths, centering yourself, and call upon Michael to guide this reflection. In your mind or aloud, say, "Archangel Michael, I ask for your presence to help me clarify my true goals. Reveal to me the desires that align with my highest path." As you speak, feel Michael's energy surrounding you, a calming blue light that brings peace to your mind and clarity to your heart.

With Michael's presence beside you, allow your mind to settle into a reflective state. Begin to consider what goals or desires feel most genuine and meaningful to you. These may relate to your career, relationships, health, personal growth, or spiritual path. As each goal arises in your mind, ask yourself if it aligns with your true self, if it feels expansive, energizing, and purposeful. Michael's presence helps you to distinguish desires rooted in true purpose from those shaped by fleeting wishes or external pressures.

Once you have identified a goal that feels aligned, write it down, capturing it in clear, simple language. This written statement becomes an anchor for your intention, a physical representation of your desire. As you write, visualize Michael standing beside you, his energy infusing your words with strength and clarity, reinforcing your commitment to this goal. Feel his light amplifying your intention, transforming it into a focused energy that resonates throughout your being.

To initiate the manifestation process, create a **vision** of your goal as though it is already realized. Close your eyes, and in your mind's eye, visualize the fulfillment of this goal in vivid detail. Imagine yourself in the moment where your desire has come to life. Observe the feelings of joy, gratitude, and satisfaction that arise within you. Visualize Michael's blue light surrounding this vision, illuminating it with his protection and strength. This vision is more than a mental exercise; it is an energetic alignment, a moment where you connect with the reality of your goal and bring its energy into your present experience.

To ground this vision in reality, use **affirmations** that express your faith in its manifestation. Examples include: "I am aligned with my highest path and purpose," "I am worthy of achieving my dreams with Michael's guidance," and "My goals unfold with grace and divine timing." Speak these affirmations each day, allowing them to reinforce your belief in your ability to manifest your desires. Each affirmation acts as a bridge, bringing your goal from the realm of thought into the realm of reality, supported by Michael's energy.

In addition to visualization and affirmation, a powerful practice for manifesting with Michael's guidance is the **Blue Flame of Intentional Action**. This flame represents the energy of both intention and follow-through, a balance of vision and grounded steps. Visualize a blue flame in front of you, its light steady and vibrant. Into this flame, place the essence of your goal, seeing it as a symbol that represents your desire—perhaps an object, word, or color that resonates with you. As you place this symbol into the flame, feel it transforming, absorbing the power of Michael's energy.

Now, ask Michael for guidance on the actions that will bring this goal into reality. In your mind or aloud, say, "Archangel Michael, reveal the steps I must take to manifest this goal. Guide me toward the choices that will bring this vision to life." Open yourself to any impressions, thoughts, or ideas that arise. Michael's guidance may come as subtle nudges, feelings, or realizations that lead you to specific actions. Trust these insights, knowing that Michael's wisdom aligns you with the path that best supports your goal.

To reinforce your commitment, use **Michael's Sword of Clarity** to cut through any doubts, distractions, or limiting beliefs that may hinder your progress. Visualize Michael standing beside you, holding his sword with its blade glowing in blue light. See him using this sword to cut through any thoughts or energies that create self-doubt, fear, or hesitation. With each cut, feel yourself freeing from these limitations, a weight lifting as Michael's sword clears the way for your intentions to flow without obstruction.

In moments of uncertainty or challenge, call upon **Michael's Shield of Resilience** to protect and support your efforts. Manifesting goals often requires perseverance, a steady commitment that withstands setbacks and doubts. Visualize a blue shield surrounding you, a boundary of strength that keeps discouragement and negativity at bay. Imagine Michael reinforcing this shield, making it resilient and impenetrable. This shield becomes a source of courage, a reminder that Michael's energy is with you, guiding you forward even when challenges arise.

An important part of the manifestation process is practicing **gratitude** for each step of progress. Gratitude is a powerful force that reinforces your connection with Michael's energy and amplifies the flow of manifestation. At the end of each day, take a moment to reflect on any small steps or signs of progress related to your goal. Offer gratitude for each of these moments, recognizing them as signs that your goal is unfolding. In your mind or aloud, say, "Thank you, Archangel Michael, for guiding me closer to my dreams and for the blessings along the way." This gratitude affirms your trust in the process, inviting more opportunities and alignment.

Throughout this journey, keep a **journal of manifestation**, a dedicated space to record your intentions, insights, and milestones. Use this journal to capture any ideas or guidance that Michael provides, noting specific actions or realizations that arise. This record becomes a powerful tool, allowing you to witness your progress and maintain focus. Each entry serves as a reaffirmation of your commitment, a visible testament to your dedication and the strength of your connection with Michael.

Finally, remember to remain **open to divine timing**. Manifestation is a process that unfolds not only through your efforts but also through the alignment of universal energies. Trust that Michael's guidance brings each step forward in the right moment, even if progress appears gradual. Be patient, knowing that every intention, visualization, and action is contributing to the realization of your goal. Michael's presence reminds you that manifestation is not just about achieving outcomes but about growing, learning, and aligning with a path that serves your highest good.

As you continue to work with Michael, you may notice subtle shifts—a greater sense of purpose, clarity, and resilience.

His energy becomes a constant support, a guiding force that helps you move through each stage of the manifestation process with confidence. With Michael's presence, you are not only empowered to bring your desires to life but to approach each goal with integrity, grounded in your true self.

At the end of each manifestation session, offer gratitude to Michael for his guidance, strength, and support. In your mind or aloud, say, "Thank you, Archangel Michael, for walking with me on this path, for your light that guides my every step, and for helping me to bring my dreams into reality." Feel his presence surrounding you, a reminder that you are supported, protected, and aligned with a higher purpose.

Through this journey with Michael, you not only manifest your goals but transform your life, aligning each desire with your soul's highest calling. His energy guides you to create a life that reflects your true self, a life of purpose, joy, and fulfillment. With each intention, each visualization, and each action, you bring yourself closer to a life empowered by Michael's unwavering support—a life where dreams become reality, guided by the light and wisdom of Archangel Michael.

Chapter 22
Cultivating Inner Peace

Cultivating inner peace with the guidance of Archangel Michael is a journey into the heart, a process that involves releasing anxieties, quieting the mind, and connecting with a deeper sense of harmony within. Michael's presence is a powerful stabilizing force, offering protection not only from external negativity but also from the internal conflicts and fears that disrupt our inner balance. By inviting his calm, steady energy into your life, you learn to establish a foundation of serenity, a place of refuge within yourself that remains constant regardless of outside circumstances.

Inner peace, as Michael teaches, is not the absence of challenges but a steady state of resilience and acceptance. It is a strength that radiates from within, empowering you to face life with confidence, even in moments of uncertainty. This peace is an anchor that grounds you, helping you to approach each day with clarity, compassion, and courage. In working with Michael to cultivate this peace, you build a sanctuary within, a sacred space where his light illuminates every corner of your being, bringing calm to both the heart and mind.

Begin by creating a practice of **daily stillness**, a time set aside to connect with Michael and ground yourself in his calming energy. Find a quiet space where you can sit comfortably, and allow yourself a few moments to settle. Close your eyes and take a few deep breaths, each one slower and deeper than the last. With each exhale, release any tension, stress, or lingering thoughts, allowing yourself to sink fully into this moment. As you breathe, call upon Michael, inviting his presence to join you. In your mind or aloud, say, "Archangel Michael, I ask for your peace to fill me. Surround me with your calm, ground my spirit, and help me find my center."

Visualize Michael appearing before you, his figure radiating a tranquil blue light that washes over you like a gentle wave. Feel this light moving through your body, dissolving any remaining tension, quieting each racing thought, and bringing a profound sense of calm. This blue light fills every cell, creating a sense of spaciousness within, a feeling of being held and supported. Allow yourself to rest in this light, absorbing Michael's peaceful energy, feeling your heart and mind becoming still and steady.

As you connect with Michael's presence, you may notice areas within where anxiety or fear lingers. Rather than resisting these feelings, gently acknowledge them, inviting Michael's light to touch these places. His energy is not one of suppression but of transformation, a force that allows you to release what disrupts your peace. Visualize any anxieties or worries as dark clouds within you, each one a collection of thoughts or feelings that create inner turbulence. With each breath, see these clouds dissolving, fading into Michael's blue light, until only a clear, peaceful space remains.

To reinforce this state of peace, use **affirmations** that anchor Michael's energy within your heart and mind. Affirmations such as, "I am filled with Michael's peace and strength," "My heart is calm and steady," and "I release all worries into Michael's care" serve as reminders of your connection to his energy. Speak these affirmations aloud or silently, allowing each word to resonate deeply, settling into your consciousness. Over time, these affirmations become more than words; they become a framework that supports your peace, a mental foundation that keeps you aligned with Michael's calm presence.

In moments when you encounter stress or chaos, **visualize Michael's Blue Shield** surrounding you, a barrier that keeps disturbances from entering your inner space. See this shield as a radiant blue sphere that encompasses you completely, a boundary that absorbs and dissolves any disruptive energies before they can reach you. This shield is not an escape from the world but a tool that allows you to engage with life from a place of calm resilience. With this shield in place, feel a renewed sense of confidence and peace, knowing that Michael's protection surrounds you, allowing you to respond to life rather than react.

One of the most profound ways to cultivate inner peace with Michael is through **heart-centered breathing**. Place your hand over your heart, and as you breathe, visualize each inhale bringing in Michael's blue light, filling your chest with warmth and tranquility. With each exhale, release any lingering worries or stress, allowing them to dissolve into the air. This simple practice connects you with the rhythm of your own heart, a center of love and calm that Michael's energy amplifies. Each breath draws his peace deeper into your being, transforming your heart into a reservoir of serenity that you can access at any moment.

In addition to these techniques, **meditation with Michael's presence** is a powerful tool for inner peace. During meditation, visualize yourself standing beside a quiet lake, with Michael beside you. The surface of the water is perfectly still, reflecting the sky above, a symbol of the calm that resides within you. Imagine Michael's hand on your shoulder, his energy flowing into you, grounding you in this moment of perfect peace. With his guidance, allow any thoughts or emotions that arise to pass like ripples on the water's surface, observing them without attachment. This meditation teaches you to find peace in stillness, to witness your inner world without being swayed by its movements.

For those moments when you need quick grounding, turn to **Michael's Sword of Clarity**. Visualize this sword cutting through any chaotic or intrusive thoughts, clearing a space in your mind where peace can settle. Imagine Michael standing beside you, using his sword to create a clear path, a mental space free from distraction or worry. This clarity allows you to refocus, to return to the present moment with a calm and steady mind.

Another powerful practice is **gratitude**, a state that invites peace into the heart by shifting focus from worry to appreciation. At the end of each day, take a few moments to reflect on the blessings in your life, however small. Offer gratitude to Michael for his guidance, his protection, and his unwavering support. In your mind or aloud, say, "Thank you, Archangel Michael, for the peace you bring to my life. I am grateful for your presence and the calm that fills my heart." This practice reinforces your connection to Michael, reminding you of the beauty and support that surrounds you, a source of peace that is always within reach.

If you find that certain situations or environments frequently disrupt your peace, establish a habit of **preparing with Michael's energy** before entering them. Before stepping into these spaces, visualize Michael's Blue Shield around you, and say a brief prayer or intention, such as, "Archangel Michael, protect my peace as I move through this space. Help me remain calm and steady, guided by your presence." This preparation serves as an energetic armor, a way to carry Michael's peace with you, ensuring that your inner calm remains unshaken.

To sustain inner peace over time, consider creating a **dedicated space for Michael's presence** within your home. This could be a small altar with a blue candle, a crystal like selenite or amethyst, or an image of Michael. Use this space as a place of retreat, a sanctuary where you can reconnect with his energy whenever needed. Each time you visit this space, light the candle, and take a few moments to sit in silence, allowing Michael's peace to fill you. This physical space becomes a symbol of your commitment to inner peace, a reminder that Michael's energy is always available to you.

As you cultivate inner peace with Michael's guidance, you may notice a shift within yourself—a resilience that allows you to face life's challenges with a calm heart and a steady mind. Michael's energy serves as a foundation, a source of strength that grounds you, helping you to remain centered even in the midst of uncertainty. This inner peace is not only a state of mind but a state of being, a quality that transforms the way you move through the world.

At the end of each practice, offer gratitude to Michael for his presence and his gift of peace. In your mind or aloud, say, "Thank you, Archangel Michael, for guiding me to peace, for your light that calms my heart and protects my mind. May I carry this peace within me, always." This expression of gratitude completes the practice, affirming your connection with Michael and your commitment to cultivating peace.

Through this journey with Michael, inner peace becomes more than a fleeting experience; it becomes a way of life, a strength that is woven into the fabric of your being. His presence teaches you that peace is not something to be found but something to be cultivated, a state that grows with each moment of calm, each breath, each act of compassion. With Michael's guidance, you are empowered to live from a place of peace, to approach each day with a heart that is open, a mind that is clear, and a spirit that is deeply grounded in serenity.

This path to inner peace with Michael transforms not only your inner world but your interactions with the world around you. As you walk in his light, you bring a sense of calm to all that you touch, radiating his peace to those you encounter, creating a ripple of harmony that extends far beyond yourself. This is the gift of Michael's guidance—a life anchored in peace, a heart unburdened, and a soul aligned with the quiet strength of his eternal presence.

Chapter 23
Connecting with the Angelic Hierarchy

Connecting with the angelic hierarchy, under the guidance of Archangel Michael, opens a pathway to a profound support network of divine beings who exist to aid, protect, and guide humanity. Michael, known as the protector and leader among angels, serves as a bridge to other members of this celestial hierarchy. His presence introduces you to a network of angels with specialized roles, each contributing unique energies and gifts to assist you on your spiritual journey. Through this connection, you build a relationship with a greater angelic presence, gaining access to wisdom, healing, and insight that go beyond individual needs and touch upon a deeper alignment with divine will.

Michael's role in facilitating your connection with the angelic hierarchy is one of guardian and guide. He ensures that these interactions occur within a protected, sacred space, where only energies aligned with your highest good may enter. With his support, you are empowered to explore and understand the roles of different angels, each of whom brings an energy that complements Michael's strength. This chapter explores how to call upon specific angels within the hierarchy, how to recognize their distinct energies, and how to build a relationship that enriches your spiritual journey.

Begin by setting an intention to connect with the angelic hierarchy. Find a quiet space where you can sit comfortably and relax. Close your eyes, take several deep breaths, and allow any tension or worries to dissolve. With each exhale, feel yourself grounding in the present moment, creating a calm, open space within. Call upon Michael to join you, asking him to act as your guide and protector during this session. In your mind or aloud, say, "Archangel Michael, I ask for your presence and guidance. Surround me with your light and protect this space as I open myself to the angelic hierarchy. Lead me to connect with the angels who serve my highest good."

As you call upon Michael, visualize his radiant blue light surrounding you, a shield that creates a sacred space for you to connect with the hierarchy. Feel his presence steadying and protecting you, ensuring that only benevolent energies are present. This protection is essential when working with the angelic realm, as it ensures that each connection you make is pure, aligned, and beneficial.

With Michael's guidance, take a moment to focus on the angels you wish to connect with. Each angel within the hierarchy has a unique role and energy signature. Some angels bring messages of healing, others offer wisdom, and some specialize in protection, creativity, or guidance through transitions. If you have a specific need or question, ask Michael to guide you to the angel most suited to support you in that area. Otherwise, simply open yourself to the angels who are aligned with your highest purpose at this time.

One of the most accessible angels within the hierarchy is **Archangel Raphael**, the angel of healing. To connect with Raphael, bring your attention to your heart, allowing yourself to breathe slowly and gently. Visualize a soft green light surrounding you, a warm, calming energy that brings healing to both body and mind. In your mind or aloud, say, "Archangel Raphael, I invite your healing presence to surround me. Bring your light into my being, and guide me toward wholeness." As you call upon Raphael, feel his energy filling you with a sense of comfort and peace, a balm that soothes and renews.

Another powerful presence within the hierarchy is **Archangel Gabriel**, the angel of communication and creativity. Gabriel brings clarity, helping you to express yourself authentically and to align with your creative purpose. To connect with Gabriel, focus on your throat chakra, the center of communication, and visualize a pure white light in this area. Say, "Archangel Gabriel, I invite your wisdom and clarity. Guide my words, inspire my creativity, and help me express my truth." As you call upon Gabriel, feel a sense of openness in your throat and mind, a clear channel through which ideas, words, and inspiration can flow freely.

If you seek transformation or support through change, call upon **Archangel Uriel**, the angel of wisdom and illumination. Uriel's energy helps bring insight during times of transition, offering understanding and the courage to release what no longer serves. Visualize a golden light surrounding you, illuminating your mind and heart. Say, "Archangel Uriel, I invite your guidance and illumination. Help me see clearly, understand deeply, and embrace transformation." With Uriel's presence, you may feel a subtle shift in perspective, a newfound clarity that brings wisdom and courage for the path ahead.

As you connect with these angels, allow yourself to notice any feelings, images, or words that arise. Each angel's energy carries a unique signature, a distinct presence that resonates in a specific way. Michael's energy, for example, often feels protective and strong, while Raphael's is soothing and nurturing, and Gabriel's is uplifting and clarifying. Take time to attune to each angel's presence, trusting your intuition to recognize these differences. By becoming familiar with their unique energies, you build a relationship that allows you to call upon them with greater ease and confidence.

To deepen this relationship, create a **daily practice of inviting the angelic hierarchy into your life**. Each morning, call upon Michael to join you, establishing a sacred space for connection. Then, take a moment to invite the angels who resonate with you to surround and support you throughout the day. You may say, "Archangel Michael, guide me and protect this day. Archangel Raphael, bring healing and peace. Archangel Gabriel, inspire clarity and creativity. Archangel Uriel, grant me wisdom and insight." This daily practice reinforces your connection to the hierarchy, creating a consistent flow of angelic support in every aspect of your life.

For a more profound experience, use **guided meditation** to explore the energies of different angels within the hierarchy. In a state of calm and stillness, visualize yourself entering a beautiful garden or sacred space. In this space, see Michael standing beside you, guiding you to meet each angel. Allow each presence to approach in turn, feeling their unique energy and presence. Notice any impressions, colors, or sensations that arise. This meditative practice builds familiarity with each angel's energy, creating a bond that strengthens over time.

As you work with the angelic hierarchy, remember that each angel carries not only specific gifts but also lessons and qualities that can support your growth. For example, Raphael's healing is often paired with lessons of self-care and compassion, while Gabriel's communication may encourage you to speak your truth. Approach each interaction with openness, allowing each angel to impart not only their support but also insights that enrich your journey.

To conclude each session, offer gratitude to each angel who joined you. In your mind or aloud, say, "Thank you, Archangels Michael, Raphael, Gabriel, Uriel, and all angels of light, for your guidance, protection, and love. I am grateful for your presence in my life." This gratitude reaffirms your connection with the hierarchy, a reminder of the support that is always available to you.

Over time, as you continue to connect with the angelic hierarchy, you may find a deeper sense of guidance and purpose emerging within you. The angels become familiar allies, companions on your path who offer wisdom, protection, and love at every step. Through this relationship, you not only gain insight and support but also deepen your understanding of your own spiritual nature, the qualities within you that resonate with each angelic presence.

The connection with the angelic hierarchy, led by Michael's guidance, transforms your journey, imbuing it with a sense of divine companionship and purpose. Through their energies, you are reminded that you are never alone, that each challenge and blessing is shared with a network of celestial beings who wish for your highest good. With Michael as your guide, you have access to a wealth of angelic support, a resource that enriches your life, empowers your growth, and illuminates your path.

Through this ongoing connection, you build a life infused with divine support and guidance, a journey where the angels walk with you, uplift you, and inspire you to live fully and fearlessly. This connection to the hierarchy is not only a gift but a partnership—a reminder that the universe itself is filled with beings of light who celebrate your progress and offer their unwavering support. In their presence, you find not only protection and wisdom but a profound peace that comes from knowing that you are loved, guided, and eternally connected to the divine through the angelic hierarchy.

Chapter 24
Ritual of Consecration to Michael

Consecrating yourself to Archangel Michael is a profound act of dedication, a commitment to walk a path aligned with divine courage, protection, and truth. This ritual of consecration is a sacred ceremony that deepens your connection with Michael, formalizing a bond that invites his energy into every aspect of your life. Through this consecration, you establish Michael as a guiding presence, a guardian of your journey, and a source of strength, wisdom, and light. This ritual marks a threshold, a moment of commitment where you invite Michael to become a constant companion on your spiritual path, offering his guidance, protection, and blessings in all that you do.

The purpose of this consecration is to affirm your intention to live in alignment with Michael's qualities—integrity, bravery, and a dedication to the highest truth. In committing yourself to his guidance, you become a vessel for his light, an expression of his qualities in the world. This consecration is not about surrendering control but about opening yourself to Michael's support, trusting that his presence will guide you toward your highest purpose and potential. Through this ritual, you pledge to embody his energy, to act with honor and courage, and to seek truth in all things.

To begin this sacred ritual, find a quiet and undisturbed space where you feel safe and at peace. Prepare items that resonate with Michael's energy, such as a blue or white candle, a piece of clear quartz or lapis lazuli, and a small bowl of water. These items serve as symbols of his presence, grounding his energy in the physical realm. Arrange them thoughtfully, creating an altar that honors his light. You may also wish to wear white or blue clothing, colors associated with purity and Michael's protective energy, as a further gesture of respect and alignment.

Once your space is prepared, sit comfortably and center yourself with a few deep breaths. As you inhale, visualize Michael's blue light filling you, and as you exhale, release any distractions or thoughts that do not serve this moment. When you feel calm and focused, call upon Michael to join you. In your mind or aloud, say, "Archangel Michael, I invite you into this sacred space. Surround me with your light, your protection, and your strength. I open my heart to you and dedicate myself to walk a path in alignment with your energy."

As you call upon Michael, visualize his presence before you, radiant and strong, surrounded by a powerful blue aura. Feel his energy filling the space, bringing a sense of calm, security, and unwavering support. This is a moment of communion, a meeting of energies where your spirit connects with his light in a profound and lasting way. Allow yourself to be fully present, open to his guidance and protection, and prepared to pledge your commitment to this sacred path.

To formalize your consecration, light the blue or white candle, a symbol of Michael's eternal light and protection. As you light the candle, say, "Archangel Michael, I light this candle in your honor. May its flame reflect your light in my heart, a beacon that guides me in truth, courage, and strength. I consecrate myself to your path and invite your presence to guide me in all that I do." Visualize the candle's flame growing stronger, its light filling the room, representing the beginning of your journey under Michael's guidance.

Next, hold the piece of crystal or stone in your hand, allowing it to serve as a physical anchor for Michael's energy in your life. Focus on the intention behind your consecration, the qualities you wish to embody with Michael's help, and the ways you seek his guidance. Say, "Archangel Michael, I consecrate this crystal as a symbol of our bond. May it hold your strength, protection, and wisdom, a reminder of my commitment to walk with you in light and integrity." Visualize Michael's energy flowing into the crystal, charging it with his presence, transforming it into a sacred talisman that you can carry with you or place on your altar.

To deepen your consecration, use **Michael's Sword of Light** as a symbol of your dedication to truth and courage. Close your eyes and visualize Michael handing his sword to you, its blade glowing with a blue-white light. This sword represents his qualities of protection and integrity, a tool that you will carry with you in spirit to guide your actions. Imagine yourself holding this sword, feeling its weight and strength in your hands, a representation of the courage and truth you commit to embody.

Say, "Archangel Michael, with your sword of light, I pledge to live in truth, to seek justice, and to protect those who cannot protect themselves. May this sword be a symbol of my commitment to walk a path of courage and integrity." As you speak, visualize the sword becoming one with your energy, merging with your spirit, a permanent symbol of your consecration to Michael's path. This act is a vow to uphold his qualities, a pledge to carry his light within you as you move through the world.

Next, take the bowl of water, a symbol of purification and renewal. Place your hands over it, and in your mind or aloud, say, "Archangel Michael, I bless this water with your light. May it cleanse me, renew me, and wash away anything that no longer serves my highest path." Dip your fingers into the water, and gently touch it to your forehead, heart, and palms, inviting Michael's energy to purify you in mind, body, and spirit. This water serves as a symbolic cleansing, a way to release any past energies, doubts, or fears that may have held you back, allowing you to begin this new path with a clear and open heart.

To seal the consecration, speak your vow of dedication. Place your hand over your heart, close your eyes, and say, "Archangel Michael, I consecrate myself to your guidance and protection. I pledge to walk in courage, to speak with truth, and to act with integrity. I invite your light into my life, and I dedicate myself to the path that aligns with your purpose. With your guidance, I vow to serve the highest good and to carry your strength in all that I do." Feel each word resonating deeply within you, a commitment that connects your spirit to Michael's light in a lasting bond.

Allow a moment of silence to follow, a space where Michael's energy can fully integrate with yours. In this silence, feel his light filling every part of your being, his presence merging with your energy. This is the essence of consecration—a union of your will with Michael's guidance, a blending of energies that solidifies your bond. You may sense a warmth, a gentle pressure, or simply a profound feeling of peace, a confirmation that Michael's presence is now a part of you, guiding and protecting you on your journey.

As you conclude the ritual, thank Michael for his presence and for accepting your consecration. In your mind or aloud, say, "Thank you, Archangel Michael, for your light, your strength, and your guidance. I honor this consecration, and I am grateful for your protection in all that I do." Extinguish the candle as a symbol of completing the ritual, knowing that Michael's light remains with you even as the flame fades.

In the days and weeks following your consecration, take time to reflect on this commitment and to integrate Michael's energy into your daily life. Keep the consecrated crystal close, perhaps wearing it or placing it on your altar as a reminder of this sacred bond. Return to your vow regularly, renewing your dedication to walk in alignment with Michael's qualities of courage, integrity, and protection. Each day, take a moment to connect with his presence, reaffirming your dedication to his path and allowing his light to guide your actions and decisions.

This consecration marks a powerful shift, a transformation that brings Michael's presence into every aspect of your life. His guidance will be with you, a source of strength, clarity, and protection that supports you in both challenges and moments of peace. Through this bond, you are empowered to live with purpose, to uphold truth and justice, and to move through life with a heart that is open, fearless, and aligned with the divine.

Consecrating yourself to Archangel Michael is a journey of dedication, a path that enriches your spirit and brings his qualities into every facet of your existence. This ritual is not only a pledge but a partnership, a way to walk through life guided by Michael's unwavering strength and light. With each day, each choice, and each act of courage, you honor this consecration, embodying Michael's essence as a beacon of hope, truth, and love in the world.

Chapter 25
Enhancing Your Angelic Communication

Enhancing communication with Archangel Michael is an invitation to deepen your relationship with him, developing the skills and practices that allow you to receive his guidance with clarity and confidence. Michael, as a powerful protector and guide, speaks through subtle energies, quiet impressions, and intuitive insights. Strengthening your ability to receive these messages opens a pathway to a profound spiritual dialogue, one where you feel his presence as a constant source of support, wisdom, and direction. Developing angelic communication with Michael transforms your connection from occasional glimpses into an ongoing relationship, a bond that informs your daily choices and actions.

The journey of angelic communication is one of attunement—learning to quiet the mind, open the heart, and trust in the subtleties of divine energy. Michael's messages may come in many forms, from sensations and symbols to dreams and synchronicities. By enhancing your communication with him, you create a channel through which his guidance flows more freely, enabling you to navigate life with his protection and insight close at hand.

To begin developing this communication, first cultivate an atmosphere of **receptivity** within yourself. Find a quiet space and set the intention to connect with Michael. Sit comfortably, close your eyes, and take a few deep breaths, grounding yourself in the present moment. As you breathe, imagine any distracting thoughts or worries dissolving, creating a calm and open space within your mind. In your heart, invite Michael's presence to join you. In your mind or aloud, say, "Archangel Michael, I open my heart to your guidance. Help me to hear your voice, to feel your presence, and to receive your messages with clarity and trust."

As you invite him, visualize a brilliant blue light surrounding you, a protective and calming energy that connects you with his presence. Feel his light filling you, bringing a sense of peace and security that allows you to open yourself fully to his guidance. This light creates a channel, a sacred space where his messages can be felt, heard, and understood without interference from doubts or distractions.

A powerful practice for developing angelic communication is **intuition training**. Michael's guidance often arrives as intuitive insights—a sudden knowing, a feeling, or a mental image that appears unbidden. To strengthen this intuitive channel, begin by paying close attention to subtle feelings or impressions that arise in response to a question or situation. Start with simple questions, such as "What do I need to focus on today?" or "What will help me feel grounded?" Take a moment to tune into the first feeling, thought, or image that arises, trusting that this is Michael's way of communicating with you.

As you practice this intuition training, you may notice a particular feeling or sensation that often accompanies Michael's guidance—a warm sensation, a light pressure on your shoulder, or a gentle tingling in your hands. These sensations are Michael's energetic signature, signs that his presence is with you and that his guidance is being transmitted. By paying attention to these physical cues, you develop a familiarity with his energy, a subtle recognition that grows stronger over time.

Journaling is another essential tool for enhancing angelic communication. Create a dedicated journal for your interactions with Michael, a place to record your impressions, insights, and any messages you receive. Begin each entry with a simple intention, such as, "Michael, I invite your guidance as I write. May your messages be clear and insightful." Then, allow your thoughts to flow freely onto the page, writing whatever comes to mind. This process often unlocks deeper layers of understanding, allowing Michael's messages to emerge in unexpected ways. Journaling creates a record of your communication, enabling you to look back and notice patterns, themes, or recurring symbols that may have initially gone unnoticed.

Meditation with **visualization techniques** is also an effective way to enhance your communication with Michael. Begin by closing your eyes, grounding yourself with a few deep breaths. Visualize yourself standing in a sacred space, perhaps a serene garden or a temple filled with light. In this space, imagine Michael approaching, his presence radiant and calm. See him standing beside you, a reassuring figure of strength and wisdom. In this visualization, ask him a question or request his guidance on a particular issue. Open yourself to whatever images, words, or feelings arise, trusting that these are Michael's responses. This meditative practice creates a safe space where you can communicate freely, strengthening your connection with each session.

Another effective approach to angelic communication is learning to recognize **symbols and signs**. Michael often communicates through symbols that carry personal or universal meaning. These symbols may appear in dreams, repeated numbers, or objects that catch your attention unexpectedly. Feathers, especially blue or white, are a common symbol of Michael's presence and protection. Pay attention to these symbols when they appear, taking a moment to acknowledge Michael's message. When you notice a symbol that feels significant, pause, take a deep breath, and ask Michael to clarify its meaning. Over time, you will develop a personal lexicon of symbols, a language of communication unique to your connection with Michael.

Dream communication is another profound way to receive Michael's messages. Before going to sleep, set an intention to invite Michael's guidance into your dreams. In your mind or aloud, say, "Archangel Michael, I invite your presence in my dreams. Please reveal any guidance that serves my highest good." Keep a journal by your bedside, and upon waking, take a few moments to record any dreams, symbols, or emotions you remember. Michael's messages in dreams may be subtle or symbolic, and recording them helps you to reflect on and interpret their meaning over time.

For more immediate guidance, practice **breath-based invocation** to quiet the mind and open the heart. When you feel the need for Michael's insight or comfort, close your eyes, place a hand over your heart, and take several deep, slow breaths. With each inhale, visualize Michael's blue light filling you; with each exhale, release any distractions or concerns. Once you feel calm and centered, say in your mind, "Michael, I seek your guidance on [your question or issue]. Please help me receive your message clearly." Wait in this stillness, focusing on any thoughts, feelings, or impressions that arise. This breath-based invocation is a quick way to tune into Michael's guidance whenever you need it, a practice that strengthens your ability to receive his insights with clarity.

Trust and patience are key elements in enhancing your angelic communication. The messages you receive may not always be immediate or obvious, and developing this skill requires patience and trust in the process. Michael's presence encourages you to stay open and receptive, to allow his guidance to unfold in its own time and way. Trust that his messages will come when they are most needed, even if they arrive in unexpected forms. The more you trust in his guidance, the more open the channel becomes, creating a flow of communication that is natural and effortless.

As your connection with Michael deepens, you may feel called to establish a **sacred space** dedicated to your angelic communication. This can be a small altar with a blue candle, a crystal like lapis lazuli, or an image of Michael. Use this space as a place of quiet reflection, where you can tune into his energy and invite his messages. Light the candle, sit in stillness, and allow yourself to be present with Michael, open to any guidance he may wish to share. This sacred space becomes a touchstone, a physical reminder of your bond with Michael and a focal point for deepening your communication.

Over time, as you continue these practices, you will notice a transformation in your relationship with Michael. His messages will become clearer, his presence more tangible, and his guidance more direct. Angelic communication is a journey of attunement, a path that grows richer with each moment of connection and trust. Through this ongoing dialogue, you develop a partnership with Michael, one where his wisdom flows freely, informing your life with clarity, courage, and divine support.

At the end of each session, take a moment to express gratitude for Michael's guidance. In your mind or aloud, say, "Thank you, Archangel Michael, for your messages, your protection, and your light. I am grateful for your presence in my life." This gratitude reinforces your connection, a reminder that Michael's guidance is a gift, one that supports you in living a life of purpose and alignment.

Through this journey of enhancing angelic communication, you cultivate a relationship with Michael that is intimate, supportive, and transformative. His guidance becomes a constant companion, a source of wisdom that flows into every aspect of your life. With Michael's presence, you move forward with a heart that is open, a mind that is clear, and a spirit that is empowered by the strength of divine connection.

With each message, each insight, and each act of trust, you deepen your bond with Michael, building a life guided by his light and wisdom. This connection enriches your path, a journey where every step is supported, every question answered, and every challenge met with courage. Through this relationship, you walk in partnership with the angelic realm, a journey illuminated by the unwavering guidance and love of Archangel Michael.

Chapter 26
Aligning with the Divine Purpose

Aligning with your divine purpose through the guidance of Archangel Michael is a journey into the core of who you are, an invitation to live in harmony with the unique path that your soul has chosen. Michael's role as protector and guide makes him a powerful ally in discovering and aligning with this purpose. His energy brings clarity, courage, and discernment, helping you to strip away distractions and doubts that may obscure your true calling. By aligning with the divine purpose, you begin to live a life filled with intention, a life where each action, choice, and connection brings you closer to the heart of your spiritual journey.

To align with your purpose is to walk a path where your personal growth, contributions, and joy are all expressions of a higher plan. Michael's presence supports you in recognizing this purpose, illuminating the steps that guide you toward fulfillment and inner peace. This chapter explores how to cultivate an awareness of your divine purpose and how to strengthen your commitment to it with the support of Michael's guidance.

Begin by creating a **sacred space for reflection**, where you can tune into Michael's energy and the deeper insights of your soul. Sit comfortably and take a few deep breaths, allowing yourself to relax and quiet your mind. Call upon Michael to join you, inviting his presence to guide you as you open your heart to your divine purpose. In your mind or aloud, say, "Archangel Michael, I ask for your guidance in discovering my divine purpose. Help me to see clearly, to understand deeply, and to walk the path that aligns with my highest good."

As you call upon him, visualize Michael standing beside you, his blue light surrounding you with a sense of calm and clarity. His presence brings a steadying energy, one that allows you to open yourself fully to the insights and truths that arise. This is a moment of communion, a time when you ask to see beyond the surface, to understand the deeper intentions of your soul. Feel Michael's hand gently resting on your shoulder, his energy filling you with confidence and readiness to explore this journey.

One powerful approach to discovering your purpose is to **reflect on moments of resonance**—times when you felt deeply connected, inspired, or fulfilled. These moments often contain clues to your soul's purpose, pointing to the activities, people, or experiences that align with your true self. Begin by recalling a few of these moments, allowing each memory to come into focus in your mind. What were you doing? How did you feel? What qualities did you bring forth in these moments? As you reflect, invite Michael's guidance to help you see patterns or themes, the threads that connect these experiences.

Next, create a list of **qualities or values** that resonate deeply with you—qualities such as compassion, creativity, integrity, or courage. These values are often aligned with your purpose, representing the traits your soul is drawn to express in this life. With Michael's presence beside you, ask him to highlight the values most relevant to your path. Write them down, allowing each word to settle into your heart as a touchstone for your journey. These values act as a compass, guiding you toward experiences and actions that align with your divine purpose.

Intuition training is another effective way to attune to your purpose. Michael's messages about your purpose may come through subtle nudges, feelings, or images that arise when you consider certain paths or decisions. Begin by asking yourself a simple question related to your life path, such as, "What brings me the greatest sense of fulfillment?" or "What can I do today that aligns with my highest purpose?" Quiet your mind and notice the first impressions or feelings that arise. Trust these intuitive insights, as they are often Michael's way of guiding you toward clarity.

Visualization can also deepen your connection to your purpose. Close your eyes and envision yourself in a life where you are fully aligned with your divine purpose. Picture yourself feeling joy, peace, and fulfillment, surrounded by people and experiences that resonate with your true self. In this vision, see Michael's light surrounding you, a radiant blue aura that reinforces your commitment to this path. This visualization not only connects you to the feeling of living your purpose but also anchors your intention to bring this vision into reality.

Meditative dialogue with Michael is a powerful tool for exploring your purpose. In a meditative state, imagine sitting with Michael in a serene, sacred space. Visualize him beside you, ready to guide you with his wisdom. In this space, ask him questions about your purpose, such as, "What is my soul's mission in this life?" or "What steps can I take to align more fully with my purpose?" Be open to any images, words, or feelings that arise, trusting that Michael's answers may come in unexpected forms. This meditative practice creates a direct channel of communication, allowing Michael's guidance to reach you clearly and directly.

To support your alignment with purpose, use **affirmations** that reinforce your commitment to this path. Examples include, "I am aligned with my highest purpose," "I walk my path with courage and integrity," and "I am guided by Michael's light in all that I do." Repeat these affirmations daily, allowing them to strengthen your belief in your ability to live a purposeful life. These affirmations act as seeds, planting the intention of alignment deep within your consciousness, where they can grow and flourish over time.

Symbolic acts of dedication can also help you align with your purpose. Find a small object—a crystal, a feather, or an amulet—that represents your commitment to this journey. Dedicate it to Michael, asking him to infuse it with his light and guidance. Carry or place this object somewhere meaningful, as a reminder of your dedication to walk the path of your divine purpose. Each time you see or touch this object, reconnect with Michael's presence, reaffirming your intention to live in alignment with your soul's mission.

When moments of doubt or confusion arise, return to **Michael's Sword of Clarity** as a tool to cut through any fears or uncertainties. Visualize him standing beside you, holding his sword, its blade glowing with a clear, blue-white light. See him using this sword to cut away any doubts, fears, or distractions that cloud your understanding of your purpose. With each cut, feel yourself becoming clearer, more focused, and more aligned with your true path.

Gratitude and reflection play a vital role in strengthening your alignment with purpose. At the end of each day, take a few moments to reflect on how you honored your purpose. Offer gratitude to Michael for his guidance, acknowledging the steps you took, no matter how small, toward a life of meaning and alignment. In your mind or aloud, say, "Thank you, Archangel Michael, for guiding me closer to my purpose today. I am grateful for your light and wisdom on this journey." This practice of gratitude not only reinforces your commitment but also deepens your connection with Michael, creating a cycle of intention and reflection that keeps you aligned with your path.

For added support, consider creating a **vision board** that represents your purpose and aspirations. Fill it with images, words, and symbols that reflect your true calling, those aspects of life that resonate with your values and intentions. Place Michael's image or a blue candle on the board, a reminder of his guidance. This vision board serves as a visual reminder of your purpose, a daily touchstone that reinforces your commitment to living a life aligned with your highest path.

As you continue this journey, remember that aligning with your purpose is not a single act but an ongoing process. Each day offers new opportunities to grow, learn, and realign. With Michael's guidance, trust that every experience, even those that feel challenging or unclear, contributes to your path. His presence reminds you that your purpose is a dynamic force, one that evolves with you as you deepen in wisdom, compassion, and understanding.

In moments when you feel disconnected or uncertain, return to Michael's energy. Sit in stillness, invite his presence, and ask him to restore your sense of direction. His guidance will lead you back to your purpose, helping you to realign with your highest self. Through this ongoing connection, your life becomes a reflection of your divine mission, each step a testament to your commitment to walk with purpose, integrity, and love.

By aligning with your purpose through Michael's guidance, you build a life that is meaningful, fulfilling, and in harmony with the divine. This alignment brings clarity to your choices, courage to your actions, and a sense of peace to your spirit, knowing that you are living the life your soul intended. With Michael as your guide, you are empowered to live fully, to embrace each day with purpose, and to contribute your unique gifts to the world. This is the essence of a life aligned with purpose—a journey where every moment is infused with the light, strength, and guidance of Archangel Michael.

Chapter 27
Astral Travels with Michael's Protection

Astral travel is an experience that allows the soul to explore realms beyond the physical, an expansion of consciousness that brings deeper insight into the mysteries of existence and the spiritual dimensions. However, traveling beyond the earthly plane requires a grounded approach and a protective presence to ensure that your journey is safe and aligned with your highest good. Archangel Michael, known for his strength, guidance, and protective energy, is an ideal guardian for such explorations. With his presence, you can venture into the astral plane with confidence, knowing that his light and protection are always with you.

Michael's role as your protector in astral travel goes beyond mere safety; he provides clarity and stability, helping you navigate these realms with purpose and understanding. His energy brings a sense of security that allows you to explore freely, without fear or uncertainty. When you travel under Michael's guidance, each journey becomes an experience of growth, discovery, and profound connection to the spiritual world.

To prepare for astral travel with Michael's protection, start by creating a sacred, peaceful space where you feel comfortable and at ease. This space should be free from disturbances, with dim lighting and any items that help you feel grounded, such as crystals, a blanket, or a candle. Begin by centering yourself with a few deep breaths, allowing each exhale to release any tension, worries, or lingering thoughts. Let your mind become calm, a quiet space where you can focus on your connection with Michael.

When you feel ready, invite Michael to join you, asking him to serve as your guide and protector for this journey. In your mind or aloud, say, "Archangel Michael, I call upon you to accompany me on this journey. Surround me with your protection, guide my spirit, and help me navigate the realms beyond with clarity and strength." As you speak, visualize Michael appearing beside you, his blue light enveloping you like a shield. This light is warm and comforting, a radiant aura that will stay with you as you move into the astral plane.

To reinforce Michael's presence, light a candle, preferably blue or white, as a symbol of his protective light. As the flame begins to flicker, focus on it, imagining that its glow is an extension of Michael's energy. This flame becomes an anchor, a reminder of his presence, a symbol that grounds your awareness even as you prepare to travel beyond the physical realm. With your attention on the candle, feel your connection to Michael strengthening, a steady presence that fills you with confidence and peace.

One essential technique for astral travel with Michael is the **Blue Shield of Protection**. Before you begin your journey, visualize a sphere of bright blue light surrounding your body, a boundary that keeps you safe from any lower energies or unwanted influences. Imagine Michael's energy reinforcing this shield, making it impenetrable, a resilient cocoon that allows you to move freely yet keeps you firmly protected. With this shield in place, take a few deep breaths, feeling a sense of safety and security envelop you, knowing that Michael's protection is strong and unwavering.

As you settle into this state, begin to **raise your vibration** by focusing on feelings of peace, love, and gratitude. Astral travel is a journey of the spirit, and higher vibrational states make it easier to access the realms beyond. Visualize Michael's light merging with your own, elevating your energy until you feel light, clear, and expansive. Allow any worries or fears to dissolve, replaced by a sense of trust and openness. This elevated state prepares you for the journey, creating an energetic alignment with the realms you are about to explore.

When you feel attuned, use **guided visualization** to begin your astral journey. Imagine yourself lying down, relaxed and at peace. Visualize a cord of light extending from your body, connecting you to your physical form and to Michael's protective presence. This cord serves as an anchor, a link that keeps you grounded no matter how far you travel. In your mind, see yourself gently rising, lifting from your physical body, and moving into a vast, open space filled with light. Michael is beside you, his presence a steady, reassuring guide.

As you travel, notice any **symbols, colors, or sensations** that arise. The astral plane is rich with energies and images that carry meaning. These symbols may offer insights, messages, or guidance related to your life or spiritual path. Trust in Michael's protection as you explore, knowing that he will help you interpret and understand what you encounter. If you feel drawn to a particular place or figure, follow that inclination, allowing Michael's guidance to direct your steps.

During your travels, Michael's **Sword of Light** can be a valuable tool for clearing any lower energies or entities that may appear. If you encounter a presence or energy that feels dense, dark, or unwelcome, visualize Michael's sword illuminating the space around you, cutting through any negativity and dissolving it into light. This sword acts as a beacon of clarity and purity, ensuring that your journey remains aligned with your highest purpose. With each use, feel a renewed sense of confidence, knowing that nothing can disturb the peace and sanctity of your journey.

If you find yourself in an environment that feels overwhelming or confusing, call upon **Michael's Blue Flame** to ground and refocus you. Visualize this flame as a calm, steady light that surrounds you, anchoring you and bringing you back to a place of peace and clarity. This flame serves as a touchstone, a point of return if you ever feel lost or uncertain. By focusing on the flame, you can realign with Michael's energy, regaining a clear and calm perspective on your surroundings.

To end your journey, gently **return to your physical body** by focusing on your cord of light, which reconnects you with the physical realm. Visualize yourself descending slowly, moving back into your physical form, feeling each part of your body as you ground yourself. Take a few deep breaths, focusing on the weight of your body against the surface you're lying on. Michael's presence remains with you, his protective light still surrounding you as you transition back into the physical world.

When you have fully returned, take a few moments to **reflect on your experience**. Write down any images, messages, or sensations that stood out, capturing them in a journal dedicated to your astral travels. This record will help you deepen your understanding of these journeys and recognize patterns or insights that emerge over time. Michael's guidance often reveals itself gradually, and reflecting on your experiences allows you to integrate his messages more fully.

As part of your grounding process, express gratitude to Michael for his protection and guidance. In your mind or aloud, say, "Thank you, Archangel Michael, for guiding me on this journey, for your protection and your light. I am grateful for your presence and the wisdom you have shared." This gratitude reaffirms your connection with him, a reminder of the trust and partnership you share.

Over time, as you continue to practice astral travel with Michael, you may find that your experiences grow richer and more insightful. His presence becomes an anchor, a source of strength that allows you to explore with an open heart and a calm mind. Each journey deepens your connection to the spiritual realms, revealing new layers of understanding, peace, and purpose. Michael's protection empowers you to travel freely, to engage with the astral world without fear, and to discover truths that enrich your path.

Astral travel with Michael's guidance is a transformative journey, one that brings you closer to the mysteries of the universe and the depths of your own soul. With his light by your side, you are empowered to explore these realms safely, with curiosity and confidence. His presence reminds you that you are always protected, always supported, and always aligned with the highest good.

Through each journey, you strengthen your connection to the spiritual dimensions, building a life where the wisdom of the astral world flows into the physical, enriching your daily experiences. With Michael as your guide, you walk between worlds, carrying the light, strength, and insight of the astral back into the heart of your life on Earth.

Chapter 28
Facilitating Group Healings

Facilitating group healing sessions with the guidance of Archangel Michael is a powerful way to bring transformative energy into collective spaces, enabling shared intentions of healing, connection, and spiritual elevation. As the protector and leader among angels, Michael's presence offers a potent blend of strength, compassion, and alignment with divine will, making him an ideal guide for collective healing work. Through his energy, group healing becomes a harmonious and unified experience, where individual energies align toward a shared purpose, amplifying the healing potential for everyone involved.

Group healing with Michael's guidance is an act of service that not only uplifts those present but also creates ripples of peace and light that extend beyond the immediate gathering. His protection ensures that each participant is held within a space of safety, free from any disruptions or negativity that may hinder the healing process. As a facilitator, your role is to create an atmosphere where each person feels supported, encouraged, and connected, while inviting Michael to lead the session with his wisdom and grace.

To prepare for a group healing session, create a **sacred space** where participants can gather comfortably. This space should feel calming and welcoming, free from distractions and filled with items that resonate with Michael's energy, such as blue candles, crystals, or soft music. Arrange chairs or cushions in a circle to symbolize unity, allowing everyone to feel equally connected within the group. Place a representation of Michael—

perhaps a statue, picture, or crystal—in the center, as a focal point that holds the energy of his presence throughout the session.

As participants gather, begin by grounding the energy in the room with a simple breathing exercise. Invite everyone to close their eyes, take several deep breaths, and feel themselves arriving fully in the present moment. As they breathe, encourage them to release any tension, worries, or distractions, creating a calm and open space within. When everyone feels centered, call upon Michael to join the group. In a calm voice, say, "Archangel Michael, we invite you into this space. Surround us with your light, protect and guide us, and bring your healing energy into our circle."

Visualize Michael's blue light expanding outward, enveloping the entire group in a sphere of protection and peace. Imagine this light forming a cocoon that surrounds everyone, a sacred shield that holds each participant in safety and calm. This cocoon acts as a boundary, keeping out any energies that do not serve the healing intention, and allowing only love, compassion, and light to permeate the space. This protective sphere is a vital element, as it ensures that each participant can open to the healing process without fear or distraction.

Next, lead the group in a brief **intention-setting exercise**. Ask each participant to silently set a personal intention for healing, reflecting on what they hope to receive or release during the session. These intentions may be physical, emotional, or spiritual, and can be as broad or specific as needed. As each person holds their intention in their heart, visualize Michael standing at the center of the group, his light amplifying each intention, weaving them together into a unified field of healing energy.

Once intentions are set, guide the group in a **visualization of collective healing** with Michael's energy. Invite everyone to close their eyes and imagine a brilliant blue light descending from above, filling the center of the circle. See this light expanding outward, flowing gently around each person, connecting them to one another through a web of light. In this vision, each participant is held within Michael's blue light, a network of healing energy that connects and unifies the group. As the light flows, feel it dissolving any blocks, pain, or heaviness, transforming these energies into peace, clarity, and vitality.

As the visualization continues, invite participants to place a hand over their heart, connecting with Michael's healing presence within. Encourage them to imagine Michael's light filling their heart, radiating warmth, compassion, and strength. With each breath, they draw his energy deeper into their being, allowing it to flow through every cell, bringing renewal and harmony. This individual connection creates a foundation for the collective energy, a personal channel through which Michael's light can flow into the group.

To enhance the healing process, consider incorporating **sound or chant**. Sound has a profound ability to unify energy and elevate vibrations. You may lead a simple chant that resonates with Michael's energy, such as repeating his name or intoning a sacred syllable like "Om." As the group chants together, imagine Michael's energy amplifying each sound, creating waves of healing that flow through each participant and into the collective field. This shared sound aligns the group's energy, strengthening the healing intention and reinforcing the connection to Michael's presence.

At this stage, Michael's **Sword of Light** can be invoked to cut through any remaining blocks or negative attachments within the group. Visualize Michael standing in the center, holding his sword high, its blue-white light radiating across the circle. See him moving his sword gently through the space, cutting away any cords or attachments that may be limiting the group's healing potential. With each cut, feel a sense of release, a lightness that clears the way for deeper healing to occur.

If specific individuals in the group are seeking healing in a particular area, consider incorporating a **focused blessing** for them. Invite participants to hold this individual in their thoughts, sending love and compassion from their hearts. Visualize Michael placing his hand over the person, his light pouring down like a gentle stream, filling them with strength and peace. This collective focus creates a powerful energy of support, amplifying Michael's healing and directing it toward those who need it most.

To conclude the session, guide the group in a **grounding exercise** to bring everyone back into their physical bodies. Ask each participant to place their feet firmly on the ground and to visualize roots extending from the soles of their feet, reaching deep into the earth. Feel the earth's steady energy flowing upward, grounding and stabilizing each person. As they focus on this grounding, invite Michael to seal the group's energy, ensuring that the healing is integrated and protected. Visualize his blue light gently fading, leaving a lingering sense of peace and calm.

Finally, offer a moment of **gratitude** for Michael's guidance and protection. In a quiet voice, say, "Thank you, Archangel Michael, for your presence in this circle, for your light and your healing. We are grateful for your support and guidance." Encourage each participant to express their own gratitude, either silently or aloud. This expression of thanks not only honors Michael's role in the healing but also reinforces the group's connection to his energy, leaving each person with a sense of completion and fulfillment.

Encourage participants to reflect on their experience, sharing any insights or sensations they felt during the session. Group healing often brings personal revelations, and sharing these experiences can deepen the sense of connection and community. Michael's energy lingers in these discussions, enriching each person's understanding of their healing journey and fostering a collective spirit of openness and trust.

Over time, as you facilitate more group healings with Michael, you may notice a growing ease and confidence in his guidance. His presence becomes a reliable anchor, a source of strength that supports each participant in their journey. With each session, you develop a deeper understanding of his energy, learning to trust the flow of healing that he brings into the group. This connection with Michael enriches the group's experience, creating a space where each participant feels seen, supported, and empowered to heal.

Facilitating group healing with Michael's guidance is a sacred responsibility, an act of service that transforms the lives of those who participate. Through his presence, you create a space of unity, compassion, and profound healing, a place where individual energies merge into a powerful collective force. Each group healing session becomes a testament to the strength of community, the power of shared intention, and the boundless support of the angelic realm.

Through this work, you bring Michael's light into the world, a beacon of hope and healing that extends far beyond the group itself. With each gathering, you strengthen the bond between participants, deepen their connection to Michael's guidance, and contribute to a ripple of healing that reaches into the world. This is the essence of group healing with Michael—a shared journey of transformation, held within the strength, protection, and love of Archangel Michael.

Chapter 29
Recognizing Michael as Messenger

Archangel Michael, revered as a protector and warrior, is also a messenger, a direct communicator of divine will who brings clarity, wisdom, and insight to those who seek alignment with a higher purpose. Recognizing Michael as a messenger invites you to open yourself to the messages he brings, messages that carry the light of truth and offer guidance on your spiritual path. As a messenger, Michael often delivers insights that cut through confusion, offering clear direction in times of uncertainty and grounding you in the presence of divine understanding. His role as a messenger transforms him from a passive protector into an active participant in your journey, helping you discern truth, navigate challenges, and deepen your connection to the divine.

Michael's messages often arrive in subtle, unexpected ways. They may appear as a feeling, a sudden understanding, or a sequence of signs that guide you toward greater awareness. His communication is not only about relaying information but also about aligning you with a sense of purpose, a path that resonates with your highest self. As you learn to recognize and interpret his messages, you create a dialogue with Michael, a partnership where his insights become a guiding force, helping you to walk in harmony with your soul's mission.

To attune yourself to Michael's role as a messenger, begin by creating a space of quiet receptivity, a moment where you can tune into his presence without distractions. Find a comfortable seat, close your eyes, and take a few deep breaths, each exhale releasing tension and inviting calm into your mind and body.

Once you feel grounded, call upon Michael to join you, inviting him to share any messages or insights that will support your path. In your mind or aloud, say, "Archangel Michael, I open myself to your guidance. Help me to recognize and understand the messages you bring. May your wisdom and clarity guide me on my journey."

As you invite him, visualize Michael standing before you, his blue light radiating a calm, steady presence that fills the space around you. This light creates a sense of peace and focus, a sacred atmosphere where his messages can be received without interference. Feel his presence aligning with your energy, opening a channel for his insights to flow through. This attunement is the foundation of your connection, a state of receptivity that allows you to notice the subtle ways in which Michael communicates.

Symbols and Signs are often Michael's chosen language for delivering messages. These may include recurring images, numbers, or objects that catch your attention in everyday life. Feathers, especially blue or white, are a common sign of Michael's presence, representing his guidance and protection. Repeated numbers, such as 111 or 444, can also signify his messages, encouraging you to pay attention to your thoughts and actions at that moment. When you encounter a symbol that feels significant, take a moment to pause, close your eyes, and ask Michael to clarify its meaning. Trust your intuition to interpret these signs, knowing that each symbol carries a unique message crafted specifically for you.

Dreams are another powerful medium through which Michael communicates. His messages in dreams may appear as symbols, scenarios, or even direct conversations that leave a strong impression. Before going to sleep, set an intention to receive Michael's guidance. In your mind or aloud, say, "Archangel Michael, I invite your presence in my dreams. Please reveal any guidance that serves my highest good." Keep a journal by your bed, and upon waking, take a few moments to record any dreams or feelings you remember. Over time, patterns or recurring themes may emerge, offering deeper insight into the messages Michael is conveying.

Meditation is an effective practice for opening yourself to Michael's messages. In a meditative state, you quiet the mind, creating a clear space where his insights can come through unfiltered by the noise of daily thoughts. Begin by closing your eyes, breathing deeply, and imagining yourself sitting in a serene, sacred place. See Michael standing before you, his energy surrounding you with protection and strength. In this quiet space, ask Michael for guidance on a specific question or simply invite him to share whatever message he feels is most important for you at this time. Be open to any images, words, or sensations that arise, trusting that they are Michael's way of communicating with you.

Another valuable tool for recognizing Michael's messages is **journaling**. This practice allows you to capture thoughts, impressions, and ideas that may initially seem subtle but reveal deeper meaning over time. Begin by setting an intention for your journal entry, such as, "Michael, I invite your guidance as I write. Help me to receive and understand your messages." Let your thoughts flow freely onto the page, noting any phrases, symbols, or feelings that stand out. As you continue to write, you may find that insights and understandings unfold, messages that Michael is gently revealing through your own words. Reviewing these journal entries can help you see connections and recognize the themes in his guidance.

When you seek immediate guidance, **breath-based invocation** is a simple yet effective way to connect with Michael's messages. Close your eyes, place your hand over your heart, and take a few deep breaths, focusing on the rhythm of your inhale and exhale. With each breath, imagine Michael's light filling your heart, opening you to receive his guidance. Once you feel centered, mentally ask your question or invite Michael to share any message he wishes to convey. In the stillness that follows, pay attention to any thoughts, feelings, or sensations that arise, trusting that Michael's presence is working through them to guide you.

Intuitive listening is another way to recognize Michael's messages. Often, his guidance appears as a gentle inner voice or a sudden thought that feels calm, clear, and wise. To cultivate this intuitive listening, practice tuning into your inner awareness, paying attention to the subtle differences between your own thoughts and those that feel like a direct insight from Michael. His messages will often carry a distinct sense of peace and clarity, an energy that resonates deeply and seems to come from outside your usual thought patterns. Trust these moments, allowing his insights to unfold naturally.

Michael's **Sword of Clarity** can also be used as a tool to discern his messages. When faced with confusion or conflicting thoughts, visualize Michael's sword, its blade shining with a brilliant blue-white light. See him using this sword to cut through the confusion, clearing a space of truth where his message can come through clearly. With each cut, feel a sense of mental clarity and focus, a place where you can receive his guidance without distraction or doubt.

If you encounter challenging situations or difficult decisions, call upon **Michael's Shield of Protection** to create a safe mental and emotional space for reflection. Visualize this shield surrounding you, a protective boundary that keeps out any fears, doubts, or external pressures that may cloud your perception. With this shield in place, you can focus solely on Michael's guidance, receiving his messages in a space that is calm, clear, and fully aligned with your highest good.

As you deepen your ability to recognize Michael's messages, you may begin to notice a pattern—a thread of guidance that weaves through your life, connecting moments of clarity, synchronicity, and insight. Michael's role as a messenger is not limited to specific answers but often involves guiding you toward a larger understanding, helping you see the interconnectedness of your experiences and the purpose behind them. Each message, each sign, is a step on this path, leading you closer to a life lived in alignment with divine will.

To honor Michael's role as a messenger, make a habit of **expressing gratitude** for his guidance. After each session of communication, take a moment to thank him for the messages he has shared, whether they were clear insights or subtle impressions. In your mind or aloud, say, "Thank you, Archangel Michael, for your guidance, your wisdom, and your presence in my life. I am grateful for the messages you share and the light you bring to my path." This gratitude not only strengthens your connection with him but also reinforces your openness to future messages.

Recognizing Michael as a messenger enriches your journey, offering a continuous flow of divine insight that guides your choices, actions, and growth. His messages bring clarity to moments of doubt, strength to times of challenge, and a sense of purpose to your life's unfolding. Through this partnership, you learn to trust in the gentle yet powerful wisdom he offers, knowing that each message is a gift that illuminates the path before you.

In embracing Michael as a messenger, you create a life where divine guidance is a constant companion, a source of support and understanding that infuses every moment with meaning. His presence becomes a touchstone, a reminder that you are always connected to a higher wisdom, always guided by a light that seeks only your highest good. Through each message, each insight, and each sign, Michael's role as a messenger becomes a cherished part of your spiritual journey—a journey guided by truth, protected by love, and illuminated by the unwavering presence of Archangel Michael.

Chapter 30
Dedicating Yourself to a Spiritual Mission

Dedicating yourself to a spiritual mission with Archangel Michael as your guide is a profound act of alignment, a commitment to live in harmony with your highest purpose and contribute to the greater good. Michael, known as the archangel of courage, strength, and divine will, assists those who seek to step fully into their spiritual mission with clarity and dedication. His energy empowers you to overcome obstacles, release doubts, and embrace a path that brings purpose, fulfillment, and service to others. With Michael's guidance, dedicating yourself to a spiritual mission becomes not just a personal journey, but a contribution to the world, a way to bring light and healing to those around you.

Your spiritual mission is unique, a calling that resonates with the deepest parts of your soul. It may manifest as a form of service, a creative endeavor, a path of healing, or simply living each day in alignment with compassion and integrity. Whatever form it takes, your mission reflects the gifts, values, and wisdom that your soul has chosen to bring into this life. Through dedication to this path, you live with intention, each action an expression of your highest self and a step toward fulfilling the purpose your soul came to embody.

To begin your dedication to a spiritual mission, create a sacred space where you can connect with Michael's energy and focus on your intentions. Sit comfortably, close your eyes, and take a few deep breaths, allowing your mind to settle and your heart to open. Call upon Michael, inviting his presence to guide and support you as you set the foundation for your mission. In your mind or aloud, say, "Archangel Michael, I ask for your guidance in discovering and dedicating myself to my spiritual mission. Help me to see clearly, to act courageously, and to serve with love and integrity."

As you invite Michael's presence, visualize him standing beside you, surrounded by a radiant blue light. His presence brings a sense of strength, clarity, and unwavering support, a reminder that he will walk with you on this journey, helping you overcome any fears or obstacles that may arise. Feel his energy filling the space, creating an atmosphere of calm and purpose that centers you in readiness for the mission that lies ahead.

To gain clarity on your spiritual mission, reflect on **moments of deep fulfillment or inspiration** that have touched your life. These moments often contain clues to your soul's purpose, guiding you toward the activities, people, or values that resonate most with your true self. Recall these experiences in detail—what were you doing, how did you feel, and what qualities did you embody in those moments? As you bring these memories to mind, ask Michael to highlight any patterns or themes, helping you to see the ways in which these experiences connect to your mission.

Another way to connect with your mission is to **identify your core values and strengths**. Take time to reflect on the qualities that feel most important to you—such as compassion, truth, creativity, or resilience. These values are often directly linked to your mission, representing the essence of what your soul wishes to express in this life. Write down these qualities, allowing each word to serve as a touchstone for your journey. With Michael's presence beside you, ask him to help you understand how these values can be woven into your mission, guiding you to express them through acts of service, creation, or healing.

To deepen your understanding, ask Michael to reveal any **spiritual gifts or abilities** that are part of your mission. These gifts may include intuitive insights, healing abilities, artistic talents, or even an ability to inspire others through kindness and wisdom. Hold the intention to discover these gifts and say,

"Archangel Michael, help me to recognize my spiritual gifts and understand how they support my mission." Be open to any images, words, or sensations that arise, trusting that Michael is guiding you to see the gifts that are uniquely yours to share with the world.

Once you have a clearer sense of your mission, perform a **ritual of dedication** to formalize your commitment. Begin by lighting a blue or white candle as a symbol of Michael's presence, a reminder that his light will guide you every step of the way. Place your hands over your heart and close your eyes, connecting with the intention to dedicate yourself to your mission. In your mind or aloud, say, "Archangel Michael, I dedicate myself to my spiritual mission. I commit to living with purpose, to serving with love, and to embodying the highest qualities of my soul. With your guidance, I pledge to walk this path with courage and integrity."

As you speak, visualize Michael standing before you, holding his Sword of Light. Imagine him using this sword to trace a circle of light around you, sealing your dedication and creating a sacred boundary that holds your mission in protection and strength. This circle represents your commitment, a space where you can grow and fulfill your purpose without interference from doubt or negativity. Feel the energy of this commitment settling within you, grounding you in a sense of purpose that is both expansive and deeply rooted.

For ongoing support, establish a **daily practice of connection with Michael** to reinforce your dedication. Each morning, take a moment to invite his presence, setting an intention to align with your mission. Place your hand over your heart and say, "Archangel Michael, guide me to act with purpose today, to live in alignment with my mission, and to serve with love and truth." This daily dedication keeps you connected to your purpose, a gentle reminder that each action, no matter how small, contributes to the fulfillment of your mission.

Gratitude and reflection are essential practices for maintaining alignment with your mission. At the end of each day, take a few moments to reflect on the ways in which you honored your mission, whether through an act of kindness, a moment of insight, or simply staying true to your values. Offer gratitude to Michael for his guidance, acknowledging his role in helping you fulfill your purpose. In your mind or aloud, say, "Thank you, Archangel Michael, for guiding me on my mission, for your strength, and for your light. I am grateful for your support and presence."

If challenges arise along the way, use **Michael's Sword of Light** to cut through any doubts or obstacles that may impede your path. Visualize Michael standing beside you, holding his sword, its blade glowing with a brilliant blue-white light. See him using this sword to cut through any fears, distractions, or external pressures that cloud your sense of purpose. With each cut, feel yourself becoming clearer, more focused, and more aligned with your mission. This act serves as a reminder that you have the strength and clarity needed to stay true to your path.

For times of uncertainty, Michael's **Blue Shield of Protection** can provide comfort and stability, especially when the demands of your mission feel challenging. Visualize his shield surrounding you, a barrier that keeps out any negative influences or doubts. This shield allows you to remain steady and committed, even when facing difficulties. With Michael's protection, you can focus solely on your mission, grounded in the knowledge that you are supported and guided.

As you continue to live in dedication to your mission, you may notice a transformation within yourself—a deeper sense of fulfillment, a clarity of purpose, and a quiet strength that sustains you through every challenge and triumph. Michael's presence becomes a source of unwavering support, a reminder that you are never alone in your pursuit of a life aligned with divine will. Each day spent honoring your mission brings you closer to the heart of who you are, an embodiment of the love, wisdom, and light that Michael inspires in you.

Dedicating yourself to a spiritual mission is a profound journey of growth, service, and self-discovery. With Michael as your guide, you walk this path with courage, purpose, and a sense of connection to something greater than yourself. His presence is a constant companion, a source of protection, guidance, and encouragement that strengthens your commitment to live in alignment with your soul's purpose.

Through each act of service, each moment of integrity, and each choice to stay true to your mission, you bring Michael's light into the world, a reflection of the divine purpose that you are here to fulfill. With Michael's support, your spiritual mission becomes more than a personal journey; it becomes a beacon of hope and love that radiates outward, touching lives, uplifting spirits, and contributing to the healing of the world.

This is the essence of dedicating yourself to a spiritual mission with Archangel Michael—a life lived in alignment, a path walked in faith, and a journey supported by the strength and wisdom of the divine. Through this dedication, you embrace your role as a bearer of light, a soul committed to the highest good, forever guided by the unwavering presence of Archangel Michael.

Chapter 31
Attaining Spiritual Ascension

Spiritual ascension is the process of elevating one's consciousness to higher levels of awareness, alignment, and understanding. It is a journey of releasing lower energies, expanding into divine wisdom, and embodying your highest potential. With Archangel Michael as a guide, the path of ascension becomes one of profound transformation, marked by his protection, strength, and clarity. Michael's role in ascension is to help you transcend limitations and fears, illuminating a path that leads toward unity with your true self and the divine source. His energy serves as a steady anchor that grounds your spiritual growth, allowing you to expand safely and purposefully.

The journey of ascension is not one of escaping the physical world but of embracing a fuller reality, where the spiritual and physical merge harmoniously. Michael's guidance brings clarity to each step, helping you release what no longer serves you and cultivate qualities that reflect your divine essence. This chapter explores advanced practices for spiritual ascension, each one designed to raise your vibration, expand your awareness, and deepen your connection to divine truth, all while staying aligned with Michael's protective presence.

Begin your ascension work by setting a strong foundation in **intentional alignment** with Michael's energy. Find a quiet, sacred space where you can center yourself without distractions. Sit comfortably, close your eyes, and take a few deep breaths, allowing each exhale to release any tension or scattered thoughts. Invite Michael to join you, setting the intention to align fully with your highest path. In your mind or aloud, say, "Archangel Michael, I call upon you to guide me in my journey of ascension. Surround me with your protection, ground me in your strength, and lead me toward the highest expression of my soul."

As you speak, visualize Michael's blue light surrounding you, a protective aura that both grounds and elevates your energy. Feel his presence anchoring you, creating a safe space where you can release old patterns and expand into new levels of awareness. This blue light is a reminder that no matter how high your consciousness rises, Michael's guidance will keep you stable and clear.

One of the core practices for spiritual ascension is **meditative elevation**—a meditation technique that helps raise your vibration and connect with higher realms of consciousness. Begin by visualizing yourself surrounded by a golden light, a radiant energy that represents divine love and wisdom. As you breathe, feel this golden light expanding, lifting you gently toward higher levels of awareness. Imagine Michael standing beside you, his energy interwoven with yours, acting as a stabilizing force that keeps you balanced as you ascend.

In this elevated state, you may experience feelings of peace, unity, or a heightened sense of clarity. Allow these sensations to flow through you, trusting that Michael's presence keeps you grounded. When you feel ready, gently return your focus to your physical body, bringing with you any insights or sensations from this higher realm. This practice of meditative elevation helps you acclimate to higher vibrations, allowing you to integrate these energies gradually and with Michael's support.

Clearing lower energies is a crucial step in ascension, as it frees you from attachments and patterns that may hold you back. Visualize Michael standing before you, holding his Sword of Light, its blue flame illuminating the space around you. See him using the sword to cut away any cords, attachments, or negative energies that linger in your field. With each cut, feel a sense of liberation, a release from the weights of the past. This cleansing creates space for higher frequencies to enter, aligning you with your ascended self and clearing any energies that no longer serve your path.

To anchor these higher energies, practice **embodying divine qualities** with Michael's guidance. Choose qualities that resonate with your ascended self, such as compassion, wisdom, courage, or love. As you focus on each quality, invite Michael to amplify it within you. For example, if you choose compassion, visualize a radiant pink light in your heart, expanding with each breath. Imagine Michael's light merging with this pink glow, strengthening and deepening your capacity for compassion. This practice is not only an act of embodiment but an alignment with the essence of ascension—a state where your inner qualities reflect the divine.

Chakra alignment and activation are essential for maintaining a high vibrational state during ascension. With Michael's guidance, work through each chakra, beginning at the root and moving upward. For each chakra, visualize a vibrant light in the corresponding color, expanding and clearing any blockages. As you move through each chakra, invite Michael's light to merge with your own, harmonizing and elevating your energy centers. This alignment creates a smooth, open channel for divine energy to flow through you, supporting your ascension journey with balance and clarity.

In times of energetic intensity, **grounding with Michael's Blue Shield** is essential to stay centered. Ascension can sometimes bring feelings of dizziness, disorientation, or even anxiety as your energy adjusts to higher frequencies. To ground yourself, visualize Michael's Blue Shield surrounding you, a steady and resilient barrier that keeps you anchored to the earth. Feel the energy of this shield stabilizing you, creating a sense of calm and security that allows you to process higher energies without feeling overwhelmed.

During your ascension journey, you may encounter moments of spiritual insight or visions. Michael's **Sword of Clarity** is invaluable for discerning these experiences and understanding their true meaning. When you receive a vision or message, visualize Michael's sword illuminating the scene, cutting through any confusion or misinterpretation. With his guidance, allow yourself to perceive the truth behind each experience, discerning what aligns with your path and releasing anything that feels unclear or misaligned.

To deepen your connection with the divine source, **heart-centered meditation** with Michael can elevate your consciousness and open you to profound spiritual insights. Place your hand over your heart and visualize a small blue flame within, a spark of Michael's energy. With each breath, feel this flame expanding, radiating warmth, love, and divine wisdom. Allow this flame to fill your entire being, lifting you into a state of unity with the divine. This heart-centered focus brings you closer to your essence, aligning you with the purest aspects of your soul's purpose.

Daily intentions are a powerful way to anchor your ascension journey. Each morning, set a simple intention to align with your highest path and to embody divine qualities. Say, "Today, I align with my highest self, guided by Archangel Michael. May I walk in love, wisdom, and truth." This intention acts as a reminder of your commitment to ascension, helping you to bring spiritual awareness into every moment and action. With Michael's support, this intention becomes a grounding point, a touchstone that guides your day and keeps you aligned with your spiritual goals.

Reflecting on your progress is another essential element of the ascension journey. Each day, take a moment to acknowledge any insights, growth, or shifts in perception you've experienced. Offer gratitude to Michael for his guidance, expressing thanks for each step he has helped you take. In your mind or aloud, say, "Thank you, Archangel Michael, for guiding me on my path of ascension. I am grateful for your light and for the wisdom you share with me." This gratitude strengthens your connection with Michael, reinforcing the bond that supports your journey.

Throughout the process of ascension, remain open to **inner transformation**. Michael's presence encourages you to release old identities, fears, and limitations that may no longer align with your true self. Each release is an opportunity to step closer to your highest expression, to embody a version of yourself that reflects divine truth. Trust in this transformation, knowing that Michael's guidance will help you navigate the changes with grace and strength.

As you continue on this path, you may notice a deepening sense of peace, clarity, and unity with all of life. This is the essence of ascension—an elevation of your consciousness that brings you closer to the divine source, a state where you experience life as an expression of love, wisdom, and interconnectedness. Michael's presence becomes a constant companion on this journey, a protector who holds your spirit steady as you expand into your highest self.

Attaining spiritual ascension with Michael's guidance is a journey of profound transformation, a path that leads you into the heart of your divine essence. Each practice, each moment of release, and each act of alignment brings you closer to a life of higher awareness, a life infused with purpose, peace, and unity. With Michael's unwavering support, you walk this path with courage and clarity, stepping into a state of being where you embody the divine truth of who you are.

In embracing the journey of ascension, you create a life that reflects the light, wisdom, and love of the divine source. Through each step, each insight, and each transformation, you fulfill the sacred potential of your soul, rising into a life that is guided, protected, and elevated by the eternal presence of Archangel Michael.

Chapter 32
Celebrating Sacred Festivities

Celebrating sacred festivities with Archangel Michael is an invitation to honor divine moments of spiritual significance and deepen your relationship with his protective and guiding presence. These celebrations are more than traditions; they are rituals that align you with divine rhythms, inviting Michael's strength, wisdom, and blessings into your life. Through these festivities, you reconnect with spiritual traditions that transcend time and space, paying homage to the light and purpose that Michael represents. In doing so, you create a profound sense of connection, not only with Michael but also with others who have walked this path, honoring the eternal link between the divine and humanity.

Sacred festivities can vary widely, drawing from spiritual traditions that celebrate Michael as a guardian and protector. Whether you observe traditional feast days, celestial events, or moments of personal significance, each occasion is an opportunity to invite Michael's energy into your life with intention and gratitude. This chapter will guide you through various ways to celebrate these sacred moments, offering practices and rituals that honor Michael's presence and open channels for his blessings.

One of the most universally celebrated feast days for Archangel Michael is **Michaelmas** on September 29. This day, also known as the Feast of the Archangels, is a time to honor Michael as a defender of truth and a source of divine protection. Begin the day by setting up an altar dedicated to Michael. Include items that resonate with his energy, such as a blue candle, crystals like lapis lazuli or selenite, and images of Michael. You might also include symbols of strength and courage, such as a small sword or a feather, to represent his qualities.

As you light the candle, invite Michael's presence into your space, saying, "Archangel Michael, I honor you on this sacred day. May your light protect, guide, and bless me." Feel his energy surrounding you, his light filling the room with a sense of peace and strength. Take a few moments to reflect on Michael's qualities and his role in your life, allowing his energy to inspire you as you go about your day. This simple act of intention sets a tone of reverence and invites Michael's blessings into your celebration.

A key ritual for Michaelmas is **the Sword of Light Blessing**. Visualize Michael's sword, a glowing blade of blue-white light, extending into your own hands. This sword represents courage, truth, and divine protection. Hold the intention that Michael's sword will guide you to stand in your truth and act with integrity. Say, "With Michael's Sword of Light, I pledge to walk a path of courage and honor. May his strength be with me in all that I do." This blessing is an affirmation of your connection to Michael's strength, a commitment to embody his qualities in your own life.

Another powerful way to honor Michael during sacred festivities is to perform a **fire ceremony**. Fire, as a symbol of transformation and divine power, resonates with Michael's energy. If safe and practical, light a small bonfire or a ceremonial candle outdoors. Stand before the flame, visualizing Michael's presence in the light. As you gaze into the flame, release any fears, doubts, or burdens that you wish to surrender. Say, "Archangel Michael, I release all that no longer serves me into your light. May your fire transform and renew my spirit." Feel a sense of purification, as if Michael's energy is clearing away the old, creating space for renewal and growth.

During these sacred festivities, consider creating a **prayer of dedication** to Michael. Write this prayer in a journal or on a piece of paper that you place on your altar. This prayer can be a simple expression of your gratitude and reverence, as well as a request for Michael's continued guidance and protection. An example might be: "Archangel Michael, I dedicate my path to your guidance. May your light guard my steps, your wisdom guide my choices, and your courage fill my heart. I honor your presence in my life and invite your blessings upon this sacred day."

Certain celestial events, such as the **equinoxes and solstices**, also hold spiritual significance and serve as meaningful times to honor Michael's guidance. The equinox, when day and night are equal, symbolizes balance and can be celebrated with Michael's energy of justice and harmony. During an equinox, create a simple ritual of balance by lighting two candles—one to represent the light and one for the dark. Invite Michael to bless this balance in your life, saying, "Archangel Michael, I seek balance within and around me. Guide me in harmony, bringing light to the shadows and peace to my soul." This ritual is an offering of alignment, a way to honor Michael's role as a balancer of energies.

The **winter solstice** can be another deeply spiritual occasion to celebrate with Michael's presence. As the longest night of the year, it symbolizes the return of light, a powerful metaphor for Michael's protective and illuminating presence. On this night, light a blue candle and sit in quiet reflection, welcoming the promise of light that follows the darkest hour. Visualize Michael's light growing within you, filling you with hope and strength. Say, "Archangel Michael, as the light returns, may your presence guide me through all that is dark. Be my light in every moment, my strength through every challenge."

Personal milestones, such as birthdays or the anniversary of a significant event, can also serve as sacred moments to honor Michael's guidance in your life. On these days, create a ritual of gratitude, acknowledging the role Michael has played in your journey. Write a letter to him, expressing your thanks for his protection, strength, and wisdom throughout the past year. Reflect on moments when you felt his presence, and offer your commitment to continue walking with his guidance. Place the letter on your altar, allowing it to serve as a reminder of your connection and dedication.

For any sacred festivity, consider performing a **meditative communion** with Michael. Begin by sitting quietly, closing your eyes, and inviting his presence into your heart. Visualize Michael as a radiant figure of light before you, his energy calm, strong, and loving. In this meditative state, ask him to share any messages, insights, or blessings he wishes to offer. Be open to any images, sensations, or words that arise, trusting that Michael is communicating directly with your spirit. This communion allows you to deepen your relationship with him, bringing his blessings into your consciousness in a personal and meaningful way.

As you conclude each festivity, offer gratitude for Michael's presence. In your mind or aloud, say, "Thank you, Archangel Michael, for joining me in this celebration. I honor your guidance, your protection, and your light in my life." This gratitude serves as a closing to the ritual, a respectful acknowledgment of the blessings and insights Michael has shared with you. With this closing, you honor both the sacred occasion and the ongoing relationship you have with him.

Sacred festivities with Michael bring a sense of purpose, peace, and divine connection to the moments you choose to celebrate. Each ritual, blessing, and prayer is a step deeper into the sacred bond you share with him, a path that invites his presence not only on special days but in every aspect of your life. These festivities create a spiritual rhythm, a series of moments where the divine enters the everyday, reminding you of the light, protection, and guidance that Michael provides.

As you continue to celebrate these sacred moments with Michael, you may find that his presence becomes more tangible, his guidance more intuitive, and his protection more readily felt. Through each festivity, you strengthen your connection to the divine, creating a life where spiritual celebration and divine guidance are woven into the fabric of your everyday experience.

These sacred moments are not isolated; they are part of a continuum, a journey where every celebration, every prayer, and every intention brings you closer to the divine purpose you share with Archangel Michael.

Through these celebrations, you walk a path illuminated by his light, a path where your spirit rises to meet the divine in love, reverence, and unity. This is the essence of celebrating sacred festivities with Michael—a journey of honoring, connecting, and opening yourself to the eternal presence of Archangel Michael, a journey that enriches your spirit and brings his blessings into the world.

Chapter 33
Exploring Esoteric Teachings

Exploring the esoteric teachings associated with Archangel Michael opens the door to ancient wisdom, sacred knowledge, and hidden truths about the nature of the divine and the role of angels in human evolution. Michael, as a powerful spiritual figure across various mystical traditions, carries meanings and lessons that go beyond his role as protector and warrior. His presence has been revered not only in traditional religious contexts but also in mystical teachings that view him as a guide in spiritual awakening, transformation, and cosmic alignment. By delving into the esoteric aspects of Michael, you enter a deeper realm of understanding, one where the layers of his symbolic presence reveal profound insights into the mysteries of existence.

The esoteric teachings of Michael extend far beyond his role in battles against darkness; they depict him as a bridge between the physical and spiritual realms, a guardian of spiritual truth, and a force that supports humanity's journey toward enlightenment. Understanding these aspects invites you to view Michael not just as a protector but as a teacher, a wise guide who illuminates the path of self-discovery, healing, and connection with the divine source.

To begin exploring Michael's esoteric teachings, first set an intention to open yourself to the deeper layers of his presence. Find a quiet, comfortable space where you can reflect without interruption. Close your eyes and take a few deep breaths, releasing any distractions. As you breathe, invite Michael to guide you into the heart of his mysteries, saying, "Archangel Michael, I open myself to your ancient wisdom. Reveal to me the hidden truths, the teachings that guide my spirit toward unity and enlightenment." Feel his presence surrounding you, a calm, knowing energy that invites you to journey beyond the surface and into the depths of his esoteric nature.

One of the core aspects of Michael's esoteric teachings is his role as a **Guardian of Light and Truth**. In many mystical traditions, Michael is seen as the keeper of divine truth, a force that illuminates and guards the eternal wisdom of the universe. As the Guardian of Light, Michael's presence is said to dispel illusions, freeing the soul from attachments to false identities and worldly illusions. To connect with this aspect of Michael, engage in a practice of **self-inquiry**. Sit quietly and ask yourself questions that reveal the essence of who you are beyond societal roles and personal history. With Michael's guidance, seek to uncover the true self, the spirit that is eternal, wise, and unbound by worldly definitions.

To deepen this practice, visualize **Michael's Sword of Truth** cutting through layers of conditioning and illusion. Imagine this sword illuminating hidden aspects of your consciousness, bringing clarity and understanding. As you feel Michael's energy, allow any untrue perceptions or limitations to dissolve. This exercise, though subtle, is a powerful way to understand the deeper truths Michael represents and to embody his clarity and insight in your own journey of self-realization.

In esoteric teachings, Michael is also known as the **Guardian of the Cosmic Order**, an archangel who maintains balance and harmony between worlds. This role aligns him with the principles of universal balance, where dualities such as light and dark, creation and destruction, work together to create a unified whole. To explore this aspect, meditate on the concept of cosmic balance with Michael. Visualize him holding a radiant blue scale, a symbol of the harmonious balance that sustains the universe. Reflect on areas of your life that may be out of balance, asking Michael to help you restore equilibrium. In your mind or aloud, say, "Archangel Michael, guide me toward balance and harmony in all areas of my life. Help me align with the cosmic order and flow with divine rhythms."

This meditation on cosmic order offers a profound way to connect with Michael's role as a guardian of balance, helping you to live in harmony with universal laws and to honor the sacred cycles of creation, growth, and transformation.

Michael's connection to **sacred geometry** is another esoteric aspect of his teachings. Sacred geometry is often viewed as the blueprint of creation, patterns and symbols that reflect divine harmony and order. Many mystics associate Michael with the geometry of the hexagon, a symbol that represents balance, stability, and protection. To work with this aspect of Michael, draw a hexagon or visualize one in your mind. Imagine Michael's light filling this shape, amplifying its qualities of balance and protection. Use this symbol as a meditation focus, allowing Michael's energy to harmonize your mind, body, and spirit with the divine structure of the universe.

Another esoteric teaching associated with Michael is his role as a **guide in the process of spiritual alchemy**. Spiritual alchemy is the transformation of lower energies into higher states of consciousness, a journey of turning the "lead" of base emotions into the "gold" of spiritual wisdom and love. Michael is often seen as a mentor in this process, guiding the soul through stages of purification, insight, and transformation. To connect with this aspect, engage in a meditation of **inner alchemy** with Michael. Visualize a blue flame within your heart, a spark of Michael's energy that purifies and elevates any lower thoughts, emotions, or attachments. With each breath, see this flame growing brighter, transforming anything heavy or dark into pure light.

Through this process, Michael helps you to transmute inner challenges, fears, and limitations, guiding you toward a state of clarity and divine understanding. This journey of alchemy is not only about personal healing but also about aligning yourself with your highest spiritual potential, moving closer to the truth of who you are.

Many esoteric teachings also view Michael as a **Guardian of the Etheric Plane**, a dimension that exists between the physical and spiritual realms. The etheric plane is believed to be the realm of spiritual essence, where divine archetypes and energies reside before manifesting in the material world. As the guardian of this plane, Michael is said to help those who seek deeper understanding of their spiritual origins and purpose. To explore this aspect, use **etheric travel meditation** with Michael's protection. Begin by imagining Michael's blue light forming a shield around you, a boundary that ensures your safety. In this protected state, allow yourself to relax deeply, inviting Michael to guide your awareness into the etheric plane. Be open to any impressions, images, or sensations that arise, trusting that Michael's energy is guiding you safely through this exploration.

In some mystical traditions, Michael is also seen as a **Guardian of the Akashic Records**, the vast library of all soul experiences and knowledge across time and space. Accessing the Akashic Records is often thought to bring insights into past lives, current lessons, and future potential. To connect with Michael in this capacity, visualize a grand library filled with light. Imagine Michael standing before the entrance, a guardian who ensures that only those with pure intentions may enter. In your mind or aloud, say, "Archangel Michael, grant me access to the knowledge that will guide my highest path. Reveal to me the insights that align with my growth and truth." Allow Michael's presence to open the way, helping you to access wisdom that can illuminate your spiritual journey.

Finally, **Michael's role as a guide in the process of soul evolution** is central to his esoteric teachings. He is seen as a being who aids souls in their progression through lifetimes, helping them to learn, grow, and move toward unity with the divine. To honor this aspect, reflect on the lessons you have encountered in your life and how each has contributed to your soul's evolution. With Michael's guidance, see these experiences as part of a greater journey, a path that leads you toward spiritual wholeness. In quiet reflection, ask Michael to show you how each challenge, each success, and each moment of transformation has been part of your growth.

Exploring these esoteric aspects of Michael enriches your understanding of his presence, transforming him from a protector into a profound spiritual teacher and guide. His teachings reveal layers of divine knowledge, offering a path of growth that connects you with the mysteries of the universe and the wisdom of your own soul. By connecting with Michael in these deeper ways, you not only receive his protection but also align with the ancient wisdom he carries, wisdom that empowers you to live with clarity, strength, and purpose.

At the end of each session of exploration, express gratitude for the wisdom Michael has shared. In your mind or aloud, say, "Thank you, Archangel Michael, for revealing your ancient teachings and for guiding me on the path of truth and enlightenment. I honor your wisdom and am grateful for your light in my life." This gratitude reinforces your bond with him, a reminder of the sacred connection you share.

As you continue exploring Michael's esoteric teachings, you may notice a transformation within yourself—a deeper sense of connection, a heightened awareness, and an alignment with divine truth. His teachings encourage you to transcend the limitations of the material world, inviting you into a life guided by spiritual insight, strength, and love. Through these teachings, you walk a path illuminated by Michael's light, a journey that brings you ever closer to the divine mysteries of existence and the wisdom that lies within. This is the heart of exploring esoteric teachings with Michael—a journey into ancient knowledge, guided by a presence that transcends time and leads you toward the eternal.

Chapter 34
Honoring the Spiritual Legacy

Honoring the spiritual legacy of Archangel Michael is a journey into the timeless impact he has had on humanity's spiritual development, protection, and guidance. Michael's legacy, woven through centuries of devotion, myth, and mystery, reaches far beyond individual experiences. It encompasses the collective journey of spiritual awakening, courage, and transformation. To honor this legacy is to connect with the countless souls who have found strength, hope, and purpose through his presence, and to carry his light forward for future generations.

Michael's spiritual legacy is found across various traditions, art, scripture, and sacred sites around the world. Each depiction, story, and place serves as a vessel for his energy, an enduring testimony to his role as a divine protector, a warrior of light, and a messenger of truth. By engaging with these legacies, you deepen your understanding of Michael's spiritual mission and invite his influence into your own life. Honoring this legacy becomes both an act of remembrance and a renewal of commitment, as you allow Michael's energy to inspire your journey and uplift those around you.

Begin by connecting with **sacred symbols and artifacts** associated with Michael. Symbols such as the sword, the shield, and the blue flame are representations of his qualities—courage, protection, and transformation. Create a space in your home or meditation area where these symbols are displayed, honoring them as reminders of Michael's enduring presence. You might include a small sword replica, a blue candle, or crystals that resonate with his energy, such as lapis lazuli or selenite. Each time you approach this space, reflect on Michael's legacy, his impact on your life, and the countless others who have called upon him.

Art, particularly classical paintings and sculptures of Michael, has preserved his image as a radiant warrior of light. Engage with these depictions by visiting galleries, churches, or viewing images of Michael in art, taking time to meditate on the strength and beauty they convey. Each piece reflects humanity's reverence for Michael and his timeless role as a defender of truth. While contemplating these works, feel a connection to the artists and believers who have found inspiration in his presence. Visualize Michael's energy emanating from these images, as if he stands before you, his light unchanging through the ages.

Scripture and sacred texts, including those from Christian, Jewish, and Islamic traditions, describe Michael's divine role and his interventions. Spend time reading these passages, letting them deepen your understanding of his spiritual mission. As you read, ask for Michael's guidance to reveal the essence of these words, allowing their wisdom to resonate within you. Examples include Michael's battles against darkness, his role as a protector of souls, and his influence in moments of revelation. By engaging with these writings, you honor the spiritual teachings that have brought Michael's legacy into countless lives.

Pilgrimage to **sacred sites** dedicated to Michael can also be a powerful way to honor his legacy. Across the world, numerous shrines, chapels, and churches are dedicated to him, such as Mont Saint-Michel in France, Saint Michael's Mount in England, and the Sacra di San Michele in Italy. Visiting these sites offers a unique experience of Michael's presence, as each place carries a profound history of devotion and miracles attributed to him. As you enter these spaces, say a quiet prayer, inviting Michael to join you, honoring the many who have come before seeking his protection and guidance. Imagine his energy permeating the space, grounding you in the sacred legacy of those who have walked this path before.

If a pilgrimage is not possible, create a **virtual pilgrimage** by studying these sites and their histories, meditating on images of them, or visualizing yourself walking within their walls. In your mind, picture the intricate carvings, the glowing candles, and the quiet, powerful energy that fills these spaces. In this visualization, invite Michael to reveal his presence, honoring the continuity of devotion and faith that each sacred site represents.

Rituals of remembrance are another way to honor Michael's legacy. Light a blue candle on specific days that hold significance, such as Michaelmas, the Feast of the Archangels, or a personal day of importance. Sit in quiet reflection, inviting Michael's energy to join you, and remember the ways in which his presence has shaped your life and spiritual journey. Express gratitude for his guidance, protection, and strength. In your mind or aloud, say, "Archangel Michael, I honor your legacy, your light, and your eternal presence. May your strength and protection continue to guide and uplift all souls."

To honor Michael's legacy in a more personal way, consider acts of **service and compassion** inspired by his qualities. Michael's legacy is not limited to miraculous interventions; it also lives on in the acts of courage, kindness, and protection extended to others in his name. Volunteer at a shelter, protect those who are vulnerable, or offer comfort to those in need, embodying Michael's protective and compassionate nature. Each act of service becomes a tribute to his influence, a way of bringing his energy into the world and continuing his mission of love and protection.

Another powerful way to honor Michael's legacy is by **mentoring or guiding others** on their spiritual journeys. As Michael has guided you, consider sharing his teachings, rituals, and wisdom with others who seek his presence. Whether you lead meditation groups, facilitate healing circles, or simply share stories of Michael's influence, you contribute to the collective awareness of his spiritual mission. By supporting others in their connection to Michael, you extend his legacy, ensuring that his influence continues to reach new hearts and lives.

In addition to these practices, spend time in **personal reflection** on what Michael's legacy means to you. Sit quietly with a journal, and reflect on questions such as, "How has Michael's presence influenced my life?" "What lessons have I learned from his guidance?" and "How can I carry his legacy forward?" Allow these reflections to deepen your understanding and commitment to living in alignment with his teachings. Write down any insights, realizations, or commitments that arise, letting this process strengthen your bond with him.

To honor Michael's legacy is also to engage in **prayers and invocations for collective protection and peace**. As a guardian of the world, Michael's influence extends to global and cosmic levels. Pray for his light to shield those in conflict, protect vulnerable populations, and bring peace to areas of suffering. In your mind or aloud, say, "Archangel Michael, may your light protect all those in need, may your strength uplift those who struggle, and may your presence bring peace to our world." Each prayer serves as an offering, a way of channeling Michael's energy into collective consciousness and honoring his enduring commitment to the world.

As you continue these practices, you may find that your understanding of Michael's legacy deepens, not only as a series of teachings but as a living energy that influences your actions and worldview. His legacy becomes a guiding light, a reminder of the power of faith, courage, and divine protection. With each ritual, act of service, and prayer, you reaffirm your place within a lineage of souls who have walked with Michael, carrying his light through history and into the future.

Honoring Michael's spiritual legacy is more than a personal journey; it is a participation in a timeless story of divine guidance, a story where each person who calls upon him adds to the beauty and power of his presence. Through your reverence, devotion, and dedication, you become part of Michael's mission, a steward of his light who contributes to the spiritual upliftment of humanity.

In closing, express gratitude for the privilege of being part of Michael's legacy. In your mind or aloud, say, "Thank you, Archangel Michael, for your timeless protection, strength, and guidance. I am honored to carry your light, to share your legacy, and to walk in your presence." This gratitude completes the cycle, affirming your commitment to honor and carry forward Michael's teachings.

Through this journey of honoring Michael's legacy, you deepen your bond with him, transforming his presence from a distant archetype into a living, guiding force in your life. This legacy is more than history; it is a call to embody Michael's strength, wisdom, and compassion each day. By honoring his legacy, you contribute to a world filled with light, unity, and divine protection—a world where Michael's presence continues to inspire, protect, and uplift all who walk the spiritual path.

Chapter 35
Miracles and Divine Interventions

Throughout history, Archangel Michael has been revered as a source of divine intervention, a powerful presence capable of manifesting miracles in moments of need. Stories of Michael's miraculous aid—whether on battlefields, in moments of personal crisis, or in times of spiritual seeking—illustrate his profound commitment to humanity's well-being. To call upon Michael is to open oneself to the possibility of divine assistance, to invite his power, courage, and protection into one's life. These interventions remind us of the unseen but palpable forces of the spiritual realm that act on our behalf, ensuring that we are never truly alone.

Miracles associated with Michael often transcend physical protection; they extend to emotional healing, spiritual transformation, and moments of profound clarity. His interventions bring light where there is darkness, courage where there is fear, and a renewed sense of purpose where there was doubt. By exploring these miracles, you gain insight into the boundless ways in which Michael's energy manifests, expanding your understanding of what is possible when you invite divine intervention into your life.

To invite Michael's presence in moments of need, begin by grounding yourself and setting an intention to open to his assistance. Find a quiet space where you feel comfortable and safe. Close your eyes, place a hand over your heart, and take several deep breaths, each inhale drawing in calm, each exhale releasing any tension or fear. When you feel centered, call upon

Michael by saying, "Archangel Michael, I invite your presence. In this moment of need, I ask for your guidance, your protection, and your light. Please help me to see clearly and act with courage." This invocation is an opening—a signal that you are receptive to Michael's divine intervention.

One of the most common forms of Michael's intervention is **physical protection** in times of danger. Stories throughout history tell of Michael appearing as a figure of light, wielding his sword, defending individuals or groups in moments of mortal peril. To invite this level of protection, visualize Michael standing beside you, his sword glowing with a radiant blue flame. Imagine this sword cutting through any danger or threat, forming a protective barrier around you. In your mind or aloud, say, "Archangel Michael, I ask for your shield of protection. Stand with me, defend me, and let no harm come near." Feel his presence as a powerful guardian, a force that clears the path ahead, keeping you safe from harm.

Another profound way Michael's intervention appears is through **emotional healing**. In moments of heartache, grief, or emotional pain, his energy can bring comfort, restoring inner strength and resilience. To call upon Michael's healing energy, place both hands over your heart and visualize a soft blue light enveloping you, filling you with a sense of calm and peace. Say, "Archangel Michael, bring your healing light to my heart. Help me release this pain and find strength within." Allow this light to fill every corner of your heart, dissolving any sadness or heaviness. Feel Michael's presence like a warm embrace, a reminder that you are supported, loved, and never alone.

Michael is also known to provide **guidance in times of uncertainty**, bringing clarity to situations that feel confusing or overwhelming. When seeking his guidance, sit quietly with a question or decision that weighs on your mind. Focus on this question, allowing yourself to be fully present with it. Then, imagine Michael's sword cutting through any fog of confusion, revealing a path of clarity. Say, "Archangel Michael, please illuminate my mind. Help me to see with truth and wisdom, to understand what I need to know." Open yourself to any insights or feelings that arise, trusting that Michael's wisdom is guiding you toward the right decision.

Miracles associated with Michael often involve **spiritual transformation**. In moments when you feel disconnected from your purpose or desire a deeper connection with the divine, Michael's intervention can realign you with your highest path. To invite this kind of transformation, sit quietly and visualize a blue flame within your heart, a spark of Michael's energy that grows with each breath. Say, "Archangel Michael, rekindle the fire of my spirit. Help me to live with purpose, to walk the path of my soul's highest calling." As this flame grows, feel a renewed sense of purpose, a spiritual awakening that brings clarity and commitment to your life's journey.

Michael's interventions often manifest as **synchronicities and signs** that confirm his presence and guidance. These signs may appear as repeated symbols, encounters, or messages that seem to align perfectly with your thoughts or intentions. When seeking confirmation of Michael's intervention, ask for a sign that resonates with you—a feather, a specific number, or even an unexpected encounter. Say, "Archangel Michael, if you are guiding me, please send a sign that I may recognize." Remain open and observant, trusting that Michael will answer in a way that resonates deeply, leaving you with a sense of certainty and peace.

In times of global or collective need, Michael's intervention extends beyond individuals to act on behalf of entire communities. Throughout history, Michael has been called upon as a **protector of nations** and groups, particularly in times of war or upheaval. To call upon Michael's protection for others, gather in a spirit of unity and set a collective intention for peace and protection. Visualize Michael's blue light surrounding the area, community, or group in need. Say, "Archangel Michael, we ask for your protection and peace. Surround this place with your shield, bring comfort and strength to those in need, and guard them against harm." This collective invocation invites Michael's power to act on a larger scale, bringing peace and strength to those who may be vulnerable.

Michael's interventions are often recorded as **miracles of transformation** in individuals' lives, moments when his presence catalyzes a profound shift in perspective, behavior, or understanding. Reflect on any personal experiences where you felt his presence, times when fear turned to courage, confusion to clarity, or sadness to peace. Write these moments down in a journal dedicated to your connection with Michael, recognizing them as part of his miraculous influence in your life. Revisiting these records affirms your faith in his presence and reminds you of his continuous support and guidance.

If you feel inspired, consider sharing Michael's miracles with others, especially those who may be struggling or in need of hope. Stories of his divine interventions, whether drawn from your own life or historical accounts, serve as reminders of the miracles that are possible when we invite the divine into our lives. Through sharing, you keep Michael's legacy alive, bringing his light and courage into the hearts of others who may be facing their own challenges.

To close any session of invoking Michael's intervention, offer gratitude for his presence and assistance. In your mind or aloud, say, "Thank you, Archangel Michael, for your protection, your guidance, and your miracles in my life. I am grateful for your light, your strength, and your unwavering support." This gratitude not only honors his intervention but strengthens your connection with him, affirming your openness to his guidance in all moments of need.

Miracles and divine interventions remind us of the boundless love and support that surround us, unseen but ever-present. Michael's role as a bringer of miracles is not limited to dramatic moments; it also manifests in quiet transformations, inner healings, and subtle signs that assure us of his guidance. By calling upon him with faith, you invite his light into the heart of your challenges, opening a path where his presence can work in ways that transcend the ordinary.

Through this journey of divine interventions, you deepen your relationship with Michael, transforming each request, each invocation, and each miracle into a testament of faith. His presence becomes a pillar of strength, a source of divine power that you can call upon whenever you need assistance, clarity, or protection. With Michael by your side, you learn that miracles are not rare occurrences but a natural expression of the divine's compassion and wisdom in your life.

Embracing the possibility of Michael's intervention opens you to a life touched by the miraculous, a journey where each step is protected, guided, and uplifted by his eternal presence. This is the heart of divine intervention with Michael—a sacred partnership that illuminates the path before you, bringing light to the darkest moments and strength to face any challenge that may come. Through this partnership, you walk in faith, courage, and gratitude, a life where miracles become a reflection of the divine's endless love for you.

Chapter 36
Aligning with Cosmic Cycles

Aligning with cosmic cycles through the guidance of Archangel Michael is a journey into harmony with the universal rhythms that govern creation, growth, transformation, and renewal. These cycles—reflected in the changing seasons, lunar phases, planetary movements, and celestial events—are powerful influences on both nature and the human spirit. Michael, with his protective and illuminating presence, acts as a guide in aligning with these cycles, helping you attune to the ebb and flow of cosmic energy and to harness it for your spiritual growth, healing, and transformation.

The cosmic cycles serve as reminders that life is a process of continuous change, each phase offering unique opportunities for growth and renewal. With Michael's guidance, aligning with these rhythms becomes a means of integrating divine wisdom into your daily life. His energy helps you remain grounded during moments of transition, resilient during challenges, and receptive to the new energies each cycle brings. Through this alignment, you cultivate a deeper connection with the universe and a life that flows in tune with its sacred rhythms.

Begin your journey by exploring the **seasonal cycles**. Each season has its own energy, reflected in nature's transitions from birth in spring, to growth in summer, to harvest in autumn, and rest in winter. Just as the earth moves through these phases, so too do our inner lives follow similar patterns. Take time to observe these changes in nature, recognizing the qualities each season brings. Michael's presence can help you attune to the spiritual essence of each phase, guiding you to integrate its energies.

In **spring**, the season of new beginnings, visualize Michael's light as a nurturing force that encourages the growth of new ideas, projects, or personal goals. During springtime meditation, invite Michael to help you plant the seeds of your intentions, asking, "Archangel Michael, guide me in this season of growth. Help me nurture new beginnings and support the blossoming of my highest potential." Feel his energy infusing your intentions with vitality, creating a foundation for growth in the months to come.

In **summer**, a time of abundance and expansion, connect with Michael's energy as a sustaining force that keeps your growth steady and strong. Reflect on the progress of your goals and invite Michael's light to help you maintain focus and clarity. Visualize his blue flame burning brightly, reinforcing your commitment to your path. Say, "Archangel Michael, support me in this season of abundance. Strengthen my dedication, and help me to shine brightly in alignment with my purpose."

As **autumn** arrives, the season of harvest and release, Michael's guidance becomes invaluable in helping you let go of what no longer serves you. Just as the trees release their leaves, take time to assess any beliefs, patterns, or relationships that may have fulfilled their purpose. Invite Michael's Sword of Light to assist in this release, saying, "Archangel Michael, help me to release all that I no longer need. Cut away any attachments that hold me back, and guide me to embrace the wisdom of this harvest season." This process of release clears the way for new growth and understanding.

In **winter**, a season of rest and reflection, Michael's presence provides comfort and stability. Winter is a time of turning inward, conserving energy, and gaining insight from the quiet places within. Use this time to meditate with Michael's protective light, seeking his guidance on any inner work or self-discovery. Say, "Archangel Michael, be my light during this season of rest. Help me to understand the depths within me, to find peace, and to prepare for the cycles yet to come."

Beyond the seasons, **lunar cycles** offer a powerful way to align with cosmic energy. Each phase of the moon carries a unique influence, guiding the rhythms of intention, growth, reflection, and release. To connect with the lunar cycle, start with the **new moon**, a time of setting intentions and planting seeds for new beginnings. Sit in quiet reflection and invite Michael's presence, asking him to help you set intentions that are aligned with your highest purpose. Visualize his light shining on your goals, blessing them with strength and clarity.

During the **waxing moon**, as the moon grows brighter, focus on building and nurturing your intentions. Michael's energy can serve as a protective force that sustains your growth. Imagine his presence guiding you, reinforcing your determination and helping you remain focused. Say, "Archangel Michael, sustain me as I grow. Help me stay true to my intentions and strengthen my commitment to this path."

The **full moon** is a time of illumination and manifestation, where intentions set earlier in the cycle reach their peak. During this phase, invite Michael's light to help you see any insights, truths, or blessings that have come to fruition. Sit in meditation under the full moon, visualize Michael's sword cutting through any final barriers, and say, "Archangel Michael, illuminate my path. Help me see clearly all that I have achieved and all that I still seek to manifest."

As the moon begins to **wane**, focus on release and introspection, letting go of any energies or attachments that are no longer beneficial. Use Michael's presence to help you clear these energies, preparing yourself for a new cycle. Say, "Archangel Michael, assist me in letting go. Help me release all that does not serve my highest good, and guide me to prepare for renewal."

Planetary cycles and retrogrades also play a significant role in cosmic alignment, each planet's influence touching different aspects of life. For example, during **Mercury retrograde**, a period often associated with communication challenges and reflection, Michael's energy can help you navigate this introspective phase with patience and clarity. During retrograde periods, invite Michael's wisdom to help you understand the lessons and reflections these times offer, saying, "Archangel Michael, guide me through this phase of reflection. Help me communicate with clarity and navigate this time with grace."

Celestial events, such as **eclipses, solstices, and equinoxes**, offer additional opportunities to align with cosmic energies. Eclipses, for instance, symbolize powerful shifts and revelations, moments where hidden truths may come to light. During an eclipse, create a quiet space to sit with Michael's presence, inviting him to reveal any insights or areas of your life that need transformation. Say, "Archangel Michael, guide me through this time of change. Help me to see clearly and embrace the truths that come forward." Trust his presence to help you move through these periods with courage and understanding.

The **astrological energies** of each zodiac season also offer specific themes, from Aries' courage to Pisces' intuition. Use these periods to focus on personal qualities or goals that resonate with each sign's energy. Invite Michael to guide you in embracing these qualities, whether it's the strength and independence of Aries or the compassion and spirituality of Pisces. By attuning to each sign's energy, you allow Michael's influence to amplify these qualities within you, helping you grow and expand in alignment with the cosmic flow.

To further deepen your alignment with cosmic cycles, consider keeping a **journal of your intentions, reflections, and progress** through each cycle. Documenting your experiences allows you to see patterns, track your growth, and understand how the cycles influence your spiritual path. This journal becomes a mirror of your alignment with the universe, a record of how Michael's guidance has helped you navigate each phase with wisdom and grace.

To conclude each alignment practice, offer gratitude to Michael for his guidance and protection. Say, "Thank you,

Archangel Michael, for guiding me through the cycles of life and the rhythms of the cosmos. I am grateful for your presence, your light, and your wisdom." This expression of gratitude honors Michael's role in helping you stay connected to these cycles, reinforcing your bond with him and affirming your commitment to live in harmony with the universe.

Aligning with cosmic cycles is an invitation to move with the natural rhythms of life, guided by Michael's unwavering support. Each cycle—whether of the moon, the seasons, or the planets—offers unique opportunities for growth, renewal, and transformation. With Michael as your guide, you learn to navigate these cycles with purpose, wisdom, and resilience, finding strength in his presence as you embrace each phase.

Through this journey of cosmic alignment, you deepen your connection to the universe, experiencing life as a dance of divine rhythms and cycles. Michael's presence transforms each phase into a sacred passage, one that brings you closer to your own essence and to the wisdom of the cosmos. Together, you move through life with a profound awareness of the divine order, each cycle a reflection of the spiritual journey you share with Archangel Michael.

Chapter 37
Manifesting Abundance with Michael

Manifesting abundance with the guidance of Archangel Michael is a transformative journey that goes beyond material wealth. True abundance encompasses not only financial prosperity but also emotional richness, fulfilling relationships, spiritual growth, and inner peace. Michael, with his strength, clarity, and protective presence, can assist you in releasing any blocks or limiting beliefs that stand in the way of abundance, allowing you to welcome prosperity into every area of your life. Working with Michael to manifest abundance is about aligning with the divine flow, trusting in your worthiness, and inviting blessings that resonate with your soul's purpose.

Abundance is a natural state in the universe; it flows freely where there is alignment, openness, and receptivity. Yet, blocks such as fear, self-doubt, and scarcity mindsets can hinder this flow. Michael's role in your journey to abundance is to help you recognize and release these limitations, empowering you to cultivate a mindset of gratitude, trust, and faith. Through Michael's guidance, you learn to see abundance as a reflection of divine love and support, an expression of the universe's desire to nurture and uplift you.

To begin manifesting abundance, start with a **cleansing ritual** to release limiting beliefs and energetic blocks. Find a quiet space where you feel at ease, and invite Michael to join you. In your mind or aloud, say, "Archangel Michael, I call upon your presence to help me release any blocks to abundance. Please help me clear away any fears, doubts, or beliefs that prevent me from receiving the blessings of the universe." Visualize his Sword of Light cutting through any dense or stagnant energy surrounding you, clearing the path for abundance to flow freely.

Next, engage in a **meditative visualization of abundance** with Michael. Close your eyes and imagine yourself standing in a radiant field filled with light and beauty. This field represents limitless abundance—a space where every need is met, and blessings flow freely. Visualize Michael standing beside you, his presence strong and protective. Together, see yourselves walking through this field, feeling the energy of prosperity surrounding you. Allow this visualization to expand your perception of what abundance feels like, embracing the sense of freedom, peace, and fulfillment that it brings.

An essential part of manifesting abundance is cultivating a mindset of **gratitude and trust**. Gratitude aligns you with the vibration of abundance, opening your heart to receive more. Begin each day by offering gratitude for the blessings you currently have, no matter how small. As you do this, invite Michael to help you recognize and appreciate these gifts. Say, "Thank you, Archangel Michael, for helping me see the abundance already present in my life. I trust that more blessings are on their way." This practice of gratitude strengthens your connection with Michael and aligns you with the frequency of abundance, making it easier for more to flow into your life.

Michael's **Shield of Protection** can also be used to create a secure space for your prosperity to grow. Visualize his blue shield surrounding you, a boundary that protects your energy from any external negativity or scarcity mindsets. Say, "Archangel Michael, protect my abundance. Let only thoughts and energies that support my prosperity enter my space." This protective shield allows you to maintain a positive focus on abundance, ensuring that your intentions are not disrupted by doubts or limiting influences.

Affirmations are another powerful tool in manifesting abundance with Michael's guidance. Choose affirmations that resonate with your desire for prosperity and embody a sense of gratitude, trust, and worthiness. Examples include, "I am worthy of receiving all forms of abundance," "Abundance flows to me easily and effortlessly," and "With Michael's guidance, I am aligned with the prosperity of the universe." Repeat these affirmations daily, ideally in front of a mirror, feeling Michael's presence reinforcing your words. Each affirmation is a seed planted in your consciousness, a declaration of your readiness to receive.

To amplify your manifestation efforts, create an **altar for abundance** dedicated to Michael. Include items that symbolize prosperity, such as coins, crystals like citrine or green aventurine, and a blue candle to represent Michael's light. Place a written intention on the altar, describing the abundance you wish to manifest in clear and positive terms. Light the candle each day, and as you do so, call upon Michael's guidance, saying, "Archangel Michael, I invite your blessings upon my intentions. May my life be filled with prosperity, peace, and joy."

Another powerful technique for manifesting abundance is **visualizing the flow of divine energy** into your life. Close your eyes and imagine a golden stream of light descending from above, flowing into the crown of your head and filling your body with warmth and energy. This golden light represents divine abundance, an endless source of blessings. With Michael's presence beside you, see this light expanding, filling your entire aura, and radiating outward into all areas of your life. Say, "Archangel Michael, help me receive this divine abundance with an open heart. I welcome prosperity into every area of my life."

If you encounter financial or emotional challenges, invite Michael to **cut through limiting beliefs** that may be obstructing your flow of abundance. Visualize him using his Sword of Light to dissolve any doubts or fears that hold you back. Say, "Archangel Michael, cut away any fears or limitations that prevent me from experiencing true abundance. Help me release these patterns and embrace my worthiness to receive." Feel his sword dissolving these blocks, freeing you from the chains of scarcity thinking.

In times of uncertainty, **Michael's guidance as a mentor** can help you stay focused on your abundance goals. Take a moment each day to sit quietly and connect with him, asking for insights on steps to bring more prosperity into your life. Be open to any messages, signs, or ideas that may arise, trusting that Michael's guidance will reveal practical ways to enhance your abundance. This could involve new opportunities, changes in mindset, or a fresh perspective on existing resources.

Service and generosity are also key aspects of manifesting abundance. By giving freely to others, you create a cycle of giving and receiving, amplifying the energy of abundance in your life. Practice acts of kindness, donate time or resources, or share your knowledge with those in need. Each act of generosity is a reminder of the abundance you already possess, and with Michael's support, it expands your capacity to receive even more. Say, "Archangel Michael, guide me to share my blessings generously. Help me to trust that as I give, so too shall I receive."

Finally, celebrate each **manifested blessing** as a miracle of abundance with Michael's presence. When you receive a blessing, no matter how small, pause to acknowledge and thank Michael for his role in bringing this abundance into your life. In your mind or aloud, say, "Thank you, Archangel Michael, for this gift of abundance. I am grateful for your guidance and your blessings." This gratitude strengthens your connection with him and reinforces the flow of abundance, creating a cycle of giving, receiving, and appreciating.

As you continue working with Michael to manifest abundance, you may notice a transformation in your relationship with prosperity. Abundance becomes a natural extension of your spiritual journey, a reflection of the divine love that flows freely through all of creation. Michael's presence reminds you that prosperity is not something to chase but something to welcome, an expression of the universe's infinite generosity.

Manifesting abundance with Michael is more than a quest for material gain; it is a journey of alignment, trust, and openness to the blessings that life has to offer. With his guidance, you learn to see prosperity as a state of being, one that radiates from within and attracts the resources, relationships, and opportunities that support your highest path. Through this journey, you transform abundance from an external goal into an inner state, a reflection of the boundless love and support that Archangel Michael brings into your life.

In honoring Michael's role in your journey to abundance, you open a channel for his energy to work through you, bringing prosperity, peace, and fulfillment. This is the heart of manifesting abundance with Archangel Michael—a life where blessings flow freely, where each moment is filled with gratitude, and where abundance is not merely something you seek, but something you are ready to receive. With Michael by your side, you walk a path of endless possibilities, a journey where every step is guided by his light and enriched by the blessings of the divine.

Chapter 38
Finding Support in Transitions

Times of transition, whether expected or sudden, bring both challenges and opportunities for growth. Change can disrupt comfort, test inner strength, and require new perspectives and choices. During these shifts, Archangel Michael serves as an unwavering support, offering guidance, protection, and reassurance to help you navigate these periods with grace and resilience. With Michael's presence, each transition—whether it's a career change, a personal transformation, a loss, or a new beginning—becomes a sacred passage, a time to reconnect with purpose, find inner strength, and open yourself to new possibilities.

Transitions hold the potential for profound spiritual growth, inviting you to let go of the old and embrace the unknown. Michael's guidance during these times acts as both an anchor and a source of strength, helping you to release attachments, overcome fears, and trust in the path ahead. His energy supports you in each phase, guiding you through uncertainty, preparing you for what's to come, and reminding you that you are never alone on this journey.

To connect with Michael's support during times of transition, begin by creating a quiet space where you feel centered and calm. Sit comfortably, close your eyes, and take a few deep breaths, each exhale releasing any immediate stress or tension. In your mind or aloud, say, "Archangel Michael, I call upon your strength and guidance. Stand with me as I face this change, protect my spirit, and lead me through this transition with courage and peace." Visualize Michael's presence around you, his blue light forming a cocoon of support that calms your mind and strengthens your resolve.

One powerful practice for embracing change is to engage in **Michael's Sword of Release** ritual, which helps you let go of attachments, fears, or beliefs that may hold you back during this transition. Visualize Michael standing before you, holding his radiant Sword of Light. In your mind's eye, identify anything you wish to release—whether it's fear, doubt, or past patterns—and see Michael using his sword to gently cut away these ties. Say, "Archangel Michael, help me release all that no longer serves my highest path. Free me from attachments and fears, and prepare me to move forward with trust and strength." Feel a lightness as these attachments dissolve, replaced by a renewed sense of freedom and readiness.

During transitions, fear of the unknown can create resistance. To overcome this fear, practice **visualizing a path illuminated by Michael's light**. Close your eyes and imagine standing at the beginning of a path that symbolizes your new journey. Visualize Michael walking beside you, his sword casting a blue light that illuminates the path ahead. See this light stretching forward, showing you the next few steps, even if the distant future remains unclear. Say, "Archangel Michael, illuminate my path and help me take each step with faith and courage." This visualization reminds you that you don't need to see the entire journey—only the next steps, guided and protected by Michael's presence.

Affirmations can serve as a source of empowerment and focus during transitional phases. Choose affirmations that resonate with your intention to move forward with strength, courage, and trust. Examples include, "I am open to new beginnings with courage and grace," "I release the old and embrace the new," and "With Michael's guidance, I am safe, supported, and ready for change." Repeat these affirmations daily, feeling Michael's strength infuse your words with conviction.

Each affirmation reinforces your commitment to face the transition with an open heart and a steady spirit.

Michael's **Shield of Protection** can be especially helpful when facing changes that involve external challenges or conflicts. Visualize his blue shield surrounding you, creating a boundary that protects your energy and prevents negativity or outside pressures from affecting your decisions. In your mind or aloud, say, "Archangel Michael, shield me from all distractions and negativity. Help me stay true to my path and protect my energy during this time of transition." This shield not only provides a sense of safety but also reinforces your focus, allowing you to make choices that honor your true intentions.

Reflecting with Michael on **the lessons of the past** can provide insight and guidance for your transition. Sit quietly with Michael's presence, and bring to mind past transitions you have navigated. Reflect on what you learned, how you grew, and the strengths you discovered within yourself. Say, "Archangel Michael, help me understand the wisdom of my past. Show me how these experiences can guide me in this new chapter." Trust that Michael's presence will reveal insights, helping you recognize the resilience and wisdom you carry forward.

In times of transition, **grounding rituals** with Michael's energy can bring stability and calm to your spirit. Stand with your feet firmly on the ground, and visualize roots extending from your feet into the earth, anchoring you. See Michael standing beside you, his hand on your shoulder, grounding and centering your energy. As you connect with the earth, feel any anxieties or uncertainties drain away, replaced by a sense of strength and connection to the present moment. Say, "Archangel Michael, help me stay grounded and focused as I move through this change. Let me feel the earth's support beneath me and your light guiding me from within."

If you encounter feelings of doubt or worry, use **Michael's Breath of Courage** practice to calm your mind and fortify your spirit. Take a deep breath, imagining that you are breathing in Michael's strength, courage, and resilience. With each inhale, feel his energy filling you with a deep sense of calm and confidence. With each exhale, release any fear, anxiety, or hesitation. Say, "With each breath, I draw in Michael's courage. I am strong, resilient, and ready to face this change." This breathing practice centers you in the present, reconnecting you with your inner strength and Michael's support.

During major transitions, creating a **vision board of new beginnings** with Michael's guidance can help clarify and focus your intentions. Collect images, words, and symbols that represent your goals, aspirations, and values for this new phase. As you assemble the board, invite Michael's presence, asking for his insight to guide you in choosing symbols that reflect your highest path. Say, "Archangel Michael, help me create a vision that aligns with my soul's purpose. Guide me to see my new beginning with clarity and inspiration." Place this vision board in a space where you can see it daily, serving as a reminder of the path ahead and Michael's role in supporting your journey.

For those facing the loss of a loved one, job, or significant life role, Michael's **comforting energy** provides a sense of peace and assurance. In moments of grief or uncertainty, place your hand over your heart and close your eyes. Visualize Michael standing beside you, his wings gently enveloping you in a cocoon of warmth and protection. Say, "Archangel Michael, bring me comfort in this time of loss. Help me find peace, and show me how to move forward with love and grace." Allow his energy to comfort you, filling you with a sense of acceptance and a readiness to honor what has passed while embracing the path ahead.

Transitions often bring the need for **decision-making and clarity**. When faced with choices, ask Michael for guidance in seeing the options clearly. Sit quietly with a question in your mind, and invite Michael to reveal insights that clarify your decision. Say, "Archangel Michael, help me to see the best path forward. Grant me clarity, wisdom, and the courage to make choices aligned with my highest good." Be open to any signs, feelings, or thoughts that arise, trusting that Michael is illuminating the path that resonates most with your soul's purpose.

To conclude each session of support with Michael, express gratitude for his guidance and presence. In your mind or aloud, say, "Thank you, Archangel Michael, for standing with me through this transition. I am grateful for your protection, your light, and your unwavering support." This gratitude reinforces your connection with him, honoring his role in helping you navigate each change with courage, resilience, and trust.

Working with Michael through transitions transforms each change into an opportunity for growth, insight, and renewal. His presence becomes a constant source of strength, a guiding light that helps you face the unknown with an open heart. With Michael by your side, each transition—whether challenging or exhilarating—becomes a meaningful part of your journey, a sacred passage that brings you closer to your highest potential.

In finding support with Michael during times of transition, you embrace change as a natural, empowering part of life. Through his guidance, you walk forward with courage, resilience, and a deep sense of peace, knowing that each step is protected, each decision is guided, and each moment of uncertainty is held within his light. This is the essence of navigating transitions with Archangel Michael—a journey where every change, every loss, and every new beginning is met with grace, strength, and the unwavering support of the divine.

Chapter 39
Expanding Your Multidimensional Perception

Expanding your multidimensional perception with the guidance of Archangel Michael invites you into a deeper awareness of reality, where spiritual insights and higher realms become part of your lived experience. Multidimensional perception is the ability to sense beyond the physical, to perceive energies, spiritual entities, and layers of consciousness that exist parallel to our own. It involves attuning to a greater spectrum of existence, a process that allows you to connect with higher aspects of yourself, spiritual truths, and angelic guidance. As a powerful protector and guide, Michael's presence offers a secure foundation for exploring these expanded realms, ensuring that you can navigate them with clarity and safety.

Working with Michael to cultivate multidimensional perception means gradually building your capacity to perceive energies and truths that are often hidden from the physical senses. His presence helps you to remain grounded while exploring these realms, encouraging you to expand your awareness without fear. As you develop this perception, your understanding of reality transforms, and you begin to see life as an interconnected web of spiritual, emotional, and physical dimensions, each influencing the other.

To begin expanding your multidimensional perception, create a sacred space where you feel at ease and undistracted. Sit comfortably and close your eyes, taking a few deep breaths to center yourself. Invite Michael's presence into your space by saying, "Archangel Michael, I call upon your guidance and protection. Help me to open my awareness to higher realms, to perceive the spiritual truths that surround me, and to experience these realms with clarity and safety." Feel his presence enveloping you, his blue light forming a protective boundary that holds your energy steady as you explore.

A foundational step in developing multidimensional perception is to practice **energy sensitivity exercises**. Begin by focusing on your hands, holding them a few inches apart, and imagining a sphere of light between them. Slowly move your hands closer and farther apart, noticing any sensations of warmth, tingling, or subtle resistance. This practice attunes you to the energy field around you, helping you recognize the subtle sensations of energy. Invite Michael to assist you in perceiving this energy, saying, "Archangel Michael, help me sense the flow of energy around and within me. Guide me to deepen my awareness of the subtle realms."

As you grow more comfortable with sensing energy, practice **aura visualization** with Michael's guidance. Close your eyes and visualize your aura as a field of light surrounding your body, glowing with vibrant colors. With each breath, see this aura expanding, reaching outward, and becoming brighter. Invite Michael's blue light to surround your aura, strengthening it and enhancing your perception. Say, "Archangel Michael, help me see and understand the layers of my aura. Let your light guide my vision as I explore my own energy field." With time, this practice can deepen your ability to perceive both your own aura and the auras of others.

Meditation is a powerful tool for expanding multidimensional perception, allowing you to quiet the physical senses and attune to higher realms. Begin by entering a meditative state, focusing on your breath, and allowing your mind to settle into stillness. Visualize Michael standing beside you, his presence grounding and protecting you as you open yourself to expanded awareness. Imagine yourself rising, moving gently beyond the physical, and entering a space of pure light. As you do so, invite Michael to reveal insights or energies that resonate with your spiritual growth. Say, "Archangel Michael, guide me in this journey of expanded perception. Help me to see with clarity and to connect with the truths that support my highest path."

Dream exploration is another way to access higher realms and connect with multidimensional aspects of your being. Before going to sleep, set an intention to receive insights or guidance during your dreams, asking Michael to protect and guide you throughout the night. In your mind or aloud, say, "Archangel Michael, I invite your presence in my dreams. Help me to remember and understand any messages or experiences that serve my growth." Keep a journal by your bed to record your dreams upon waking, noting any recurring symbols, themes, or feelings. Over time, you may find that your dreams become more vivid, offering glimpses into higher dimensions or deeper aspects of your psyche.

To deepen your connection with higher realms, practice **third-eye activation** with Michael's support. Sit quietly and place your focus on the space between your eyebrows, the area known as the third eye or brow chakra. Visualize a small, glowing light here, a center of perception and insight. As you focus on this light, imagine Michael's blue energy merging with it, enhancing its clarity and strength. Say, "Archangel Michael, activate my third eye, helping me to see beyond the physical and to perceive the wisdom of higher realms." Feel this center expanding, a gateway to spiritual vision that allows you to connect with subtler energies and insights.

During moments of inner stillness, experiment with **intuitive listening**, opening yourself to any messages or impressions that arise. Sit quietly with Michael's presence, clearing your mind of any distractions, and simply listen. You may notice thoughts, feelings, or subtle voices that seem to originate beyond your usual consciousness. Allow these impressions to come and go, trusting that Michael's energy is guiding you to receive insights from higher sources. Say, "Archangel Michael, help me to hear and understand the messages of the higher realms. Open my heart and mind to divine wisdom."

Working with **crystals that enhance perception** can also support your exploration of multidimensional awareness. Crystals such as amethyst, labradorite, and selenite are known for their properties of expanding consciousness and connecting with higher energies. Hold a crystal in your hand, inviting Michael's presence to amplify its properties, and place it on your third eye or hold it while meditating. Say, "Archangel Michael, bless this crystal and help it to enhance my perception. Guide me to see clearly and to connect with the wisdom of the spiritual realms." These crystals serve as tools that support your journey, creating a bridge between physical and spiritual energies.

Michael's **Sword of Clarity** is an invaluable tool for clearing away any illusions or distortions that may arise during your exploration. As you open yourself to higher realms, the mind may introduce doubts, fears, or misinterpretations. Visualize Michael holding his sword, its blue light cutting through any confusion or distractions, revealing the pure truth. Say, "Archangel Michael, use your Sword of Clarity to clear my mind of illusions. Help me to perceive the truth with wisdom and discernment." This practice strengthens your connection to Michael's energy and ensures that your perceptions remain clear and aligned with your highest good.

For added support, create a **spiritual journal** dedicated to recording your experiences, insights, and impressions as you develop your multidimensional perception. Write down any sensations, symbols, or guidance you receive, even if they seem subtle or unclear at first. Over time, patterns may emerge, offering deeper insight into your spiritual journey. Reflecting on these experiences with Michael's guidance can reveal hidden meanings and confirm the progress you're making in expanding your perception.

Finally, **express gratitude** to Michael for his guidance and protection throughout this journey of expanded perception. Each time you work with him, end the session by saying, "Thank you, Archangel Michael, for your light, your protection, and your guidance. I am grateful for the clarity and insights you bring to my path." This gratitude reinforces your bond with him, grounding your exploration in a spirit of reverence and respect.

As you continue to expand your multidimensional perception, you may find that your understanding of reality transforms, encompassing not only the physical world but also the energies, entities, and truths of higher realms. Michael's presence becomes a trusted guide in this process, helping you navigate these expanded realities with strength, clarity, and confidence. Through his guidance, you learn to trust your inner vision, embrace your spiritual insights, and explore the mysteries of existence with an open heart.

Expanding your perception with Michael is a journey into the vastness of existence, where each insight, each vision, and each impression brings you closer to the truth of who you are. His energy becomes an anchor, a grounding force that allows you to explore without fear, a reminder that you are always protected and supported. With Michael by your side, you are empowered to embrace the multidimensional nature of life, to see beyond the physical, and to connect with the divine wisdom that flows through all things.

This is the heart of expanding your multidimensional perception with Archangel Michael—a journey of awakening, discovery, and transformation, a path where you experience life as a dance of energies, colors, and truths that enrich your soul and uplift your spirit. Through this journey, you walk in the light of expanded awareness, guided by Michael's eternal presence, a being of pure love who illuminates every dimension of your spiritual path.

Chapter 40
Collaborating with Elemental Angels

Collaborating with the elemental angels under the guidance of Archangel Michael is a journey into the wisdom and energy of nature itself. The elemental angels—guardians of earth, water, fire, and air—embody the primal forces that shape our world and influence every aspect of life. Each element holds unique qualities and teachings, and by connecting with the elemental angels, you gain access to energies that support healing, balance, creativity, and personal transformation. With Michael as your guide and protector, working with these angels becomes a harmonious experience, a dance between spirit and nature that aligns you with the rhythms of the earth and the universe.

Elemental angels are not only stewards of the natural world but also allies on the spiritual path, helping you harness the powers of nature to enhance your life and deepen your spiritual practice. Collaborating with these angels through Michael's guidance invites you to honor the elements as sacred forces, to respect their wisdom, and to integrate their qualities within yourself. This collaboration expands your awareness, grounding your spirituality in the natural world and creating a sense of unity with all of creation.

To begin working with the elemental angels, create a space in your home or outdoors where you feel connected to nature. Invite Michael to join you by saying, "Archangel Michael, I call upon your guidance and protection as I connect with the elemental angels. Help me to honor and understand the wisdom of earth, water, fire, and air." Visualize Michael's blue light surrounding you, creating a sacred circle that keeps your energy grounded and aligned with your highest good. His presence assures that your connection with the elemental angels will be safe, clear, and rooted in respect.

The **earth element**, represented by the angelic beings of the earth, embodies stability, strength, and nurturing. This element is connected to physical health, abundance, and grounding. To connect with the earth elemental angels, spend time in nature, feeling the soil beneath your feet, the trees around you, and the stability of the ground. Visualize Michael's light merging with the earthy green energy of these angels, and say, "Archangel Michael and earth angels, bless me with the energy of grounding, strength, and abundance. Help me to stay rooted in my purpose and connected to the rhythms of the earth."

As you work with the earth element, notice how it brings a sense of calm and resilience, a steady foundation that supports your growth. You may also wish to carry or meditate with stones like jasper, hematite, or moss agate, which resonate with the earth's energy and strengthen your connection with these angels. The earth elemental angels encourage you to cultivate patience, nurture your body and soul, and build a life that reflects stability and abundance.

The **water element**, represented by the water elemental angels, is the force of flow, intuition, and emotional depth. This element is connected to healing, purification, and the unconscious mind. To connect with the water angels, find a body of water—such as a river, lake, or even a bowl of water in your space—and allow yourself to feel its fluidity and calm. Imagine Michael's energy joining with the soft, flowing light of the water angels. Say, "Archangel Michael and water angels, bless me with emotional healing, intuition, and peace. Help me to flow gracefully with life's changes and to listen to the wisdom within."

The water elemental angels support you in embracing your emotions, trusting your intuition, and healing past wounds. As you work with these angels, consider using water as a ritual tool, perhaps by taking a mindful bath or washing your hands with intention, symbolizing a cleansing of emotions and thoughts. With Michael's guidance, the water angels remind you of the power of fluidity, helping you navigate life's transitions and develop a deeper relationship with your inner self.

The **fire element**, represented by fire elemental angels, is the energy of transformation, passion, and creativity. Fire ignites your desires, fuels your actions, and brings forth the light of inspiration. To connect with the fire angels, light a candle or sit before a flame, feeling its warmth and vibrant energy. Visualize Michael's protective light surrounding the flame, merging with the fire angel's glowing red or golden energy. Say, "Archangel Michael and fire angels, bless me with courage, creativity, and the power to transform. Help me to embrace my passions and to act with purpose and inspiration."

Fire elemental angels encourage you to harness your inner fire, to take bold steps forward, and to release anything that no longer serves you. When working with these angels, focus on goals or dreams you wish to manifest, allowing the fire's energy to inspire and drive your actions. Through Michael's guidance, fire becomes a transformative force that fuels your soul's purpose, igniting new levels of motivation and creativity within you.

The **air element**, represented by the air elemental angels, is the energy of intellect, clarity, and communication. Air governs thoughts, ideas, and the flow of knowledge, bringing fresh perspectives and mental freedom. To connect with the air angels, spend time outdoors, feeling the wind on your skin, or simply focus on your breath as it flows in and out. Visualize Michael's presence blending with the light and transparent energy of the air angels. Say, "Archangel Michael and air angels, bless me with clarity, insight, and freedom. Help me to release limiting thoughts and to communicate with truth and wisdom."

The air elemental angels invite you to explore your mind, to seek knowledge, and to embrace a lightness of being. They help you to release stagnant ideas and bring fresh insights into your life. As you work with these angels, consider practices like journaling, deep breathing, or meditation to open your mind and heart to new perspectives. With Michael's guidance, the air angels support you in expressing yourself clearly, letting go of burdensome thoughts, and aligning with the truth of who you are.

Each elemental angel brings unique gifts, and Michael's presence provides balance and protection as you work with them. To integrate these energies into your daily life, consider creating an **elemental altar**. Place representations of each element—such as a stone for earth, a bowl of water, a candle for fire, and a feather for air—on your altar, inviting the energy of each angel into your space. With Michael's guidance, bless the altar by saying, "Archangel Michael, I invite your protection over this sacred space. May the elemental angels bring their gifts into my life, helping me to live in harmony with the natural world."

In moments when you seek balance or inspiration, use **elemental meditation** to connect with any or all of the elements. Close your eyes, and visualize Michael's blue light surrounding you, anchoring and protecting you. Then, one by one, invite each elemental angel to join you: see the green energy of earth grounding you, the blue energy of water bringing calm, the golden energy of fire igniting your passion, and the white light of air filling you with clarity. With each breath, feel these energies integrating within you, balancing your mind, body, and spirit. Say, "Archangel Michael, earth, water, fire, and air—may these elements bring balance, harmony, and inspiration to my life."

To deepen your relationship with the elemental angels, practice **gratitude and respect for the natural world**. Each time you connect with nature, whether by touching the soil, drinking water, lighting a candle, or breathing deeply, acknowledge the presence of the elemental forces and thank them for their gifts. Say, "Thank you, elemental angels, for your presence and wisdom. I honor your energy in my life and am grateful for your support." This gratitude cultivates a deep respect for the elements and reinforces your bond with these angelic forces.

Reflecting on your experiences with the elements in a **spiritual journal** can also enhance your understanding of their influence. Record any insights, feelings, or shifts in perspective that arise as you work with the elemental angels. Over time, you may notice patterns or personal growth that reveal how each element supports different aspects of your life. Michael's guidance helps you integrate these energies, allowing you to draw strength and wisdom from the natural world as you journey forward.

Collaborating with the elemental angels brings a sense of wholeness, grounding, and vitality to your spiritual path. With Michael by your side, each element becomes a doorway to greater self-understanding and connection to the divine. Earth teaches you to stand strong and nurture yourself, water guides you in emotional depth and healing, fire ignites your inner strength and creativity, and air lifts your spirit with clarity and wisdom.

In honoring the elemental angels, you open yourself to the sacredness of life, seeing the natural world as a reflection of divine intelligence and beauty. Michael's presence ensures that your journey with the elements is one of balance, respect, and harmony, guiding you to align with nature's rhythms and to recognize the interconnectedness of all things.

This is the heart of collaborating with the elemental angels under Archangel Michael's guidance—a journey of unity, empowerment, and reverence, where each element becomes a teacher, a friend, and a source of strength on your path. With Michael's support, you embrace the gifts of the earth, water, fire, and air, finding balance within and deepening your bond with the sacred forces that sustain life itself.

Chapter 41
Michael as Patron of Warriors

Archangel Michael is celebrated across cultures and spiritual traditions as a patron of warriors, a protector of those who defend justice, integrity, and peace. His role as a celestial warrior is not only a symbol of strength and courage but also a testament to his dedication to guiding and supporting those who are called to protect others. To work with Michael in this role is to invite his qualities of bravery, honor, and unshakable conviction into your own life. Whether you are facing battles in the external world or within your own heart, Michael stands beside you as an ally, offering his sword of light and shield of protection to guide you toward victory and integrity.

The concept of a "warrior" in Michael's guidance transcends physical combat; it embodies the spirit of resilience, the pursuit of justice, and the commitment to uphold truth and compassion. Those who walk this path—whether as protectors, advocates, healers, or individuals striving to overcome personal challenges—are met with Michael's steadfast presence. His energy fortifies the spirit, helping you to face challenges with a clear mind, a brave heart, and the assurance that you do not stand alone.

To begin working with Michael as a patron of warriors, create a sacred space where you can connect with his energy. Sit comfortably, close your eyes, and take a few deep breaths, each exhale releasing any tension or doubts. In your mind or aloud, say, "Archangel Michael, I call upon you as the protector of warriors. Stand with me, strengthen my spirit, and guide me in the path of justice, truth, and courage." Visualize Michael standing before you, his blue light radiating strength, his Sword of Light held high, a symbol of clarity, honor, and unbreakable resolve. Feel his energy filling you, awakening the spirit of the warrior within.

One of Michael's gifts to those who call upon him is the **Sword of Truth**. This sword represents not only physical strength but also the power of discernment, the ability to see through illusions and uphold integrity. Imagine Michael handing you this sword, its light merging with your own energy. As you hold it, feel its weight and purpose—a tool that cuts through confusion, that defends truth and clarity. Say, "Archangel Michael, bless me with your Sword of Truth. Help me to see with clarity, to speak with honesty, and to act with integrity." This visualization aligns you with Michael's strength, reminding you to seek truth and justice in all your endeavors.

Another essential aspect of Michael's guidance is his **Shield of Protection**, a symbol of defense and resilience. This shield is not only a physical barrier but also a spiritual boundary, a reminder of the importance of self-protection and inner strength. Visualize Michael's shield surrounding you, a barrier that reflects any negativity, doubt, or external pressures. Say, "Archangel Michael, protect me with your shield. Guard my spirit and help me to stand firm in my values and purpose." This shield reinforces your inner strength, creating a safe space from which you can navigate challenges with resilience and peace.

For those seeking to develop inner strength, Michael's **Breath of Courage** practice is a powerful tool. Sit quietly and place your hand over your heart, feeling your breath rise and fall. Visualize Michael's blue light entering your lungs with each inhale, filling you with courage, bravery, and confidence. With each exhale, release any fear, doubt, or hesitation. Say, "With each breath, I draw in Michael's courage. I am strong, I am protected, and I am ready to face any challenge." This breathing practice centers you, calming your mind and fortifying your spirit with Michael's unwavering strength.

Michael's role as a patron of warriors also involves helping you to overcome internal battles—struggles with fear, self-doubt, or past wounds. To work with him in this way, bring to mind any internal conflicts you wish to resolve. Visualize Michael standing beside you, his hand on your shoulder, a comforting presence that reassures you of his support. Say, "Archangel Michael, help me to conquer the battles within myself. Grant me the courage to face my fears and the strength to release what no longer serves me." Allow his energy to merge with yours, helping you to overcome these challenges and emerge stronger and more resilient.

In times of adversity, Michael's **Armor of Light** can be a powerful source of protection and empowerment. Imagine Michael placing a suit of armor made of blue and gold light around you, each piece fitting perfectly, a symbol of spiritual resilience and divine protection. Say, "Archangel Michael, shield me with your Armor of Light. Let no harm, doubt, or fear penetrate this armor. Help me to stand tall and face every challenge with courage and grace." This armor becomes a spiritual safeguard, helping you feel protected, even in the midst of difficulty, allowing you to move forward with confidence.

Affirmations of strength and resilience can reinforce your connection to Michael's warrior energy. Choose affirmations that resonate with the qualities you wish to embody, such as "I am courageous and strong," "I act with honor and integrity," or "With Michael's guidance, I overcome all obstacles." Repeat these affirmations daily, ideally while visualizing Michael's light surrounding you. Each affirmation serves as a reminder of Michael's presence, a reaffirmation of the warrior spirit that resides within you.

In times of crisis or challenge, calling upon Michael's **Intercession of Protection** can provide immediate comfort and strength. Close your eyes, focus on your heart, and visualize Michael's light surrounding you like a protective shield. Say, "Archangel Michael, I call upon your protection. Stand with me, defend me, and help me to find the strength to overcome this trial." Feel his energy anchoring you, a force that shields and strengthens, bringing a sense of peace and empowerment even in the face of adversity.

Michael also guides those who protect others—whether they are physical warriors, caregivers, advocates, or defenders of justice. If you are in a role that involves protecting or supporting others, invite Michael to stand beside you, offering his strength and guidance. Say, "Archangel Michael, guide me in my role as a protector. Help me to act with courage, compassion, and wisdom, and to honor the trust that others place in me." Feel his energy fortifying your commitment, giving you the clarity and strength needed to serve with integrity.

To honor Michael's legacy as a patron of warriors, consider creating an **altar of courage and protection** dedicated to him. Place symbols of strength—such as a small sword, a shield, or crystals like obsidian, black tourmaline, or carnelian—along with a blue candle that represents his presence. Light the candle each day and invite Michael to bless your altar, saying, "Archangel Michael, I dedicate this space to your strength and protection. May it inspire courage, honor, and resilience in all who call upon you." This altar serves as a touchstone, a place where you can reconnect with Michael's warrior energy whenever you need guidance or support.

Reflecting on your journey and the challenges you have faced can also deepen your connection with Michael's warrior guidance. In a journal, write about moments where you felt courage, times when you stood firm in your truth, or instances where you overcame adversity. Thank Michael for his role in these experiences, for his protection and guidance. Say, "Thank you, Archangel Michael, for walking beside me in every challenge. I am grateful for your strength, your courage, and your unwavering support." This reflection not only honors Michael's presence but also reinforces the warrior spirit that has grown within you.

For those who feel called to serve as advocates, protectors, or defenders in the world, Michael's guidance offers a path of purpose and resilience. His warrior spirit inspires a commitment to justice, truth, and compassion, a dedication to protecting the vulnerable and standing for what is right. As you embrace Michael's role as your patron, you align with these qualities, finding the strength to face any opposition and the courage to uphold the values you hold dear.

In honoring Michael as the patron of warriors, you walk a path of integrity, resilience, and compassion, a path illuminated by his guidance and strength. Whether you face battles in the outer world or within yourself, Michael's presence reminds you that you are never alone—that his sword, his shield, and his spirit stand beside you, helping you to overcome all that lies before you.

This is the essence of Michael's warrior guidance—a journey of courage, truth, and unbreakable faith. With Michael by your side, you face life's challenges as a spiritual warrior, a soul dedicated to the path of honor, integrity, and divine strength. Through each test, each triumph, and each moment of resilience, you embody the spirit of the warrior, a reflection of Archangel Michael's eternal light and unwavering protection.

Chapter 42
Extending the Connection to Family

Extending the connection with Archangel Michael to your family is a deeply unifying act that brings his protective, healing, and guiding presence into the hearts and lives of those you love. Family bonds, whether they are relationships by birth, choice, or spirit, form the core of our support systems, shaping who we are and who we become. Bringing Michael into these connections offers a way to strengthen family unity, healing, and understanding. His presence brings peace to conflicts, guidance in times of decision, and a shield of protection that embraces every member with love and care.

Michael's energy can uplift and unify the family unit, helping each member feel valued, protected, and connected to something greater. Working with Michael as a family not only fosters spiritual closeness but also invites a divine presence into everyday interactions, creating a harmonious atmosphere where love, respect, and compassion can flourish. Each family member, whether they are aware of his presence or not, can benefit from the light and peace that Michael brings.

To begin inviting Michael's presence into your family, start by setting a personal intention to be an anchor of his energy. Sit quietly in a comfortable space, close your eyes, and take a few deep breaths, each exhale releasing any distractions or stress. Visualize Michael standing beside you, his blue light surrounding you with warmth, protection, and peace. In your mind or aloud, say, "Archangel Michael, I invite your presence into my family. Help me to be a vessel of your peace, your protection, and your love. May your light flow through me, creating harmony and unity within my family." This intention serves as a foundation, allowing you to hold Michael's energy and share it with those you love.

Creating a family altar dedicated to Michael is a powerful way to keep his presence alive in your home. Choose a spot in a common area, such as the living room or kitchen, and place symbols that represent Michael's energy—a blue candle, images or statues of him, or crystals like sodalite, lapis lazuli, or amethyst. Encourage family members to place items of personal significance on the altar, connecting them to Michael's energy in their own unique way. Light the candle each day, and say, "Archangel Michael, we welcome your light into our home. Surround our family with your protection, your strength, and your love." This altar becomes a focal point for his energy, a place where family members can come to reconnect with his presence.

One way to strengthen family bonds with Michael's support is through **family prayers or intentions for protection and unity**. Gather together as a family and, holding hands or sitting close, invite Michael to join you. Say, "Archangel Michael, we call upon your protection and guidance for our family. Help us to support one another, to understand each other with compassion, and to find strength in unity." Each family member can take turns expressing their hopes or intentions, creating a collective prayer or intention that Michael can amplify. This practice fosters a sense of closeness and mutual support, deepening the bond that connects you all.

Individual blessings for each family member with Michael's light can help everyone feel seen, valued, and protected. Visualize each family member in turn, surrounding them in Michael's blue light. If appropriate, you may gently place your hand on their shoulder or head, silently inviting Michael's presence to bless them. Say, "Archangel Michael, bless [family member's name] with your strength, your guidance, and your protection. Help them feel safe, loved, and supported." This blessing not only strengthens their connection with Michael but also reminds them of their worth and the love that surrounds them.

Guided family meditation with Michael can bring a sense of calm and unity, especially in times of stress or change. Gather together in a comfortable space, and lead the family in a brief visualization. Close your eyes and invite each person to picture Michael's blue light surrounding the entire family, creating a warm, protective cocoon. Say, "Archangel Michael, surround our family with your peace and protection. Help us to feel your love and to connect with each other in understanding and harmony." Let this visualization create a moment of shared calm, allowing everyone to feel centered and supported.

In times of conflict or misunderstanding, Michael's guidance can bring **healing and resolution**. If a conflict arises, sit quietly with Michael's presence, asking him to help you see the situation with compassion and clarity. Visualize his light filling the space between you and the family member with whom you are struggling. Say, "Archangel Michael, bring peace to this situation. Help us to understand each other, to release any anger or fear, and to find common ground." Imagine his Sword of Light gently dissolving any tension, helping each person feel heard and respected. This practice invites Michael's energy into challenging moments, fostering empathy and reconciliation.

For families going through major transitions, such as moving, loss, or significant life changes, Michael's presence offers a sense of **stability and support**. Gather together as a family and invite Michael to help each person find strength and peace amid the change. Say, "Archangel Michael, guide us through this transition. Help us to support one another, to remain strong, and to trust in the path ahead." Visualize his light enveloping each family member, a steady force that keeps you grounded and united.

Children, in particular, can benefit from a connection to Michael's presence, finding comfort and security in his protective energy. Teach them a simple **bedtime prayer or visualization** to invite Michael to watch over them as they sleep. Guide them to imagine a blue light surrounding their bed, like a gentle cocoon, and say, "Archangel Michael, please watch over me tonight. Protect me and keep me safe." This practice helps children feel secure, knowing that they are watched over by a benevolent presence.

Involving your family in **acts of service or kindness** inspired by Michael's qualities of compassion and protection can deepen the bond between family members and expand their connection with him. Volunteer together, practice random acts of kindness, or find ways to support those in need. Say, "Archangel Michael, guide us to be vessels of your compassion and strength. Help us to bring your light to others and to work together in the spirit of love and kindness." Each act of service strengthens Michael's presence in your family, creating a shared sense of purpose and unity.

To encourage individual connections with Michael, provide family members with **small tokens or reminders** of his energy, such as a blue stone, a small medal, or a prayer card. Encourage them to carry these tokens with them or place them in personal spaces as a reminder of Michael's protection and guidance. These small items serve as touchstones, personal reminders that they are always supported by his presence.

In moments of gratitude, gather as a family to **thank Michael for his guidance and protection**. Light a candle at the family altar and, holding hands, offer words of appreciation. Say, "Thank you, Archangel Michael, for watching over our family, for your guidance, and for your love. We are grateful for your presence in our lives and for the strength you give us each day." This expression of gratitude deepens your collective connection with Michael, reaffirming the bond that unites your family in his light.

Keeping a **family gratitude journal** dedicated to Michael can also be a meaningful way to record his blessings. Encourage each family member to write or draw moments when they felt Michael's guidance, protection, or love. Over time, this journal becomes a testament to his influence, a shared record of the ways in which Michael has supported and strengthened your family.

As you continue to extend Michael's presence to your family, you may notice a shift in the energy of your home—a greater sense of peace, unity, and support. Michael's light becomes a constant presence, filling your family with love, guiding each member on their unique path, and creating a foundation of trust and strength. His influence fosters a space where everyone feels valued, understood, and supported, helping you all grow together in harmony.

In extending Michael's energy to your family, you create a legacy of love, unity, and spiritual connection that enriches each person's life. This is the essence of inviting Archangel Michael into your family—a journey where each relationship is strengthened, each heart is protected, and each soul finds peace in his presence. With Michael's guidance, your family becomes a circle of love and light, a sacred unit held together by the strength and compassion of the divine.

Chapter 43
Applying the Teachings in Daily Life

Applying the teachings of Archangel Michael in daily life is an act of weaving his strength, wisdom, and guidance into the fabric of your everyday experiences. While rituals, invocations, and meditations establish a deep spiritual connection, integrating Michael's presence into routine moments brings his energy to life in a continuous, accessible way. This chapter guides you in infusing Michael's influence into the choices, thoughts, and actions that shape your days, transforming each moment into an opportunity to align with his light and guidance. When you carry his teachings into the ordinary, you build a foundation of resilience, compassion, and clarity that supports you, not only in times of need but in the quiet, unremarkable moments that often define the course of your life.

Inviting Michael's guidance into your daily life begins with **setting intentions each morning**. Upon waking, sit quietly and place your hands over your heart, visualizing Michael's blue light surrounding you. Say, "Archangel Michael, be with me today. Guide me to act with strength, integrity, and compassion. Help me to make choices that reflect my highest self." This morning intention aligns your energy with Michael's guidance, creating a mental and emotional compass that orients your day toward clarity, protection, and purpose.

One of the most powerful ways to carry Michael's teachings into your daily life is through the practice of **mindful presence**. Michael's energy teaches us to stay grounded and fully engaged, regardless of external distractions. During your day, take moments to pause, focus on your breath, and imagine Michael's blue light filling your entire body. This practice centers you, helping you release any stress or scattered energy and return to a state of calm awareness. Say to yourself, "With Michael's guidance, I am fully present. I act with purpose, rooted in peace." Practicing mindful presence with Michael's support brings a sense of focus and purpose to even the smallest tasks, transforming them into acts of intention and clarity.

Protective visualizations are simple yet powerful ways to bring Michael's energy into situations that may be challenging or stressful. Before entering a difficult meeting, a crowded place, or any situation where you feel the need for protection, pause and visualize Michael's shield surrounding you. Picture his blue light forming a boundary that reflects any negativity or stress away from you, keeping you safe and centered. Say, "Archangel Michael, shield me with your protection. Let me move through this experience with strength, peace, and resilience." This visualization empowers you to face each situation with a calm mind and a sense of security, knowing that Michael's protective energy is surrounding you.

To apply Michael's teachings on **honesty and integrity**, commit to speaking and acting with truth throughout your day. Whenever you feel tempted to withhold your true thoughts or bend your values, remember Michael's Sword of Truth. Visualize holding this sword, its light helping you to speak with honesty and integrity. Say silently, "With Michael's guidance, I speak my truth with kindness and courage." This practice helps you to align your words and actions with your highest values, strengthening your connection to Michael's energy and building a foundation of authenticity in your relationships.

Another way to bring Michael's teachings into daily life is by practicing **acts of kindness and compassion** inspired by his protective and loving energy. Michael's presence encourages us to be a source of light for others, helping those in need and showing kindness wherever possible. Look for simple ways to serve—listening to someone who needs support, helping a friend, or simply offering a smile to a stranger. Say to yourself, "With Michael's guidance, I bring light and compassion to others." Each act of kindness becomes a living expression of Michael's energy, strengthening your bond with him and creating a ripple of positivity in the world.

In moments of self-doubt or fear, **affirmations of strength** with Michael's support can re-center your energy. Whenever you feel anxious, place a hand on your heart and silently repeat, "With Michael's guidance, I am strong, courageous, and capable." Visualize his blue light filling you with resilience, dissolving any doubts or fears. This simple affirmation helps you embody Michael's qualities, reminding you that his strength is always available to you, no matter the challenges you face.

Michael's guidance is also invaluable in cultivating **emotional balance and patience**. When you feel emotions rising—whether anger, frustration, or sadness—invite Michael's calming presence into your heart. Close your eyes, take a few deep breaths, and visualize his blue light soothing you, bringing peace to your emotions. Say, "Archangel Michael, help me to find balance within. Let me respond with patience, understanding, and calm." This practice transforms emotional reactions into conscious responses, helping you move through each situation with grace and self-awareness.

To apply Michael's teachings on **discernment and decision-making**, invite his guidance each time you face a choice, whether small or significant. Before making a decision, pause and ask Michael to help you see clearly. Visualize his Sword of Light cutting through any confusion, revealing the path that aligns with your highest good. Say, "Archangel Michael, guide me to choose wisely. Help me see with clarity and act with integrity." Trust any feelings or insights that arise, knowing that Michael's energy is illuminating the path forward.

At the end of each day, engage in a brief **reflection practice with Michael**, reviewing your day with gratitude and self-awareness. Sit quietly and invite Michael's presence, allowing his blue light to surround you. Reflect on moments when you felt aligned with his teachings, as well as any areas where you may have struggled. Say, "Thank you, Archangel Michael, for guiding me today. Help me to learn from this day and to grow stronger in your light." This practice fosters a sense of accountability and gratitude, helping you to carry his teachings forward with greater intention each day.

Keeping a **journal dedicated to Michael's influence** can also support your journey of integrating his teachings. Each evening, write down any experiences where you felt his presence, guidance, or protection during the day. Record any insights, moments of strength, or instances of kindness that felt inspired by his energy. Over time, this journal becomes a testament to his influence in your life, a record of the ways in which you are transforming through his guidance.

For physical reminders, carry a **small token of Michael's energy**, such as a blue stone, an image, or a pendant, with you throughout the day. Whenever you touch or see this token, let it remind you of his presence and of your commitment to apply his teachings. Say to yourself, "With Michael's guidance, I am protected, guided, and strong." These small reminders reinforce your connection with him, grounding you in his energy and intentions even in the busiest moments.

To conclude each day, **offer gratitude to Michael** for his guidance, support, and presence. Light a candle or sit quietly, allowing a moment to reflect on his influence in your life. Say, "Thank you, Archangel Michael, for walking with me today. I am grateful for your light, your strength, and your love. Help me to carry your teachings forward as I continue on my path." This expression of gratitude strengthens your bond with Michael, reaffirming your dedication to living in alignment with his wisdom and protection.

Incorporating Michael's teachings into daily life transforms routine actions into sacred practices, making each day an opportunity to grow, to serve, and to align more fully with your highest self. His guidance becomes a steady presence, a source of strength and peace that supports you in every choice, interaction, and experience. Through these small, intentional practices, you deepen your connection with Michael, creating a life that reflects his qualities of courage, compassion, integrity, and resilience.

Applying Michael's teachings in daily life is a journey of continuous alignment, a practice of bringing his light into the ordinary and making it extraordinary. Each moment becomes an expression of his influence, a step on a path illuminated by his presence. With Michael by your side, your days are filled with purpose, peace, and a deep sense of protection, transforming everyday life into a living reflection of his divine guidance and unwavering support. This is the heart of applying Michael's teachings—a life grounded in love, strength, and truth, a journey where each day becomes a testament to the light and wisdom of Archangel Michael.

Epilogue

The journey with Archangel Michael does not end here. Every word, symbol, and practice described in this book is a bridge, a tool for you to continue cultivating this connection in your life. Reaching this point, you have not just read but experienced a process of self-discovery and empowerment, guided by a force that transcends the material, a force that protects you and inspires you to keep moving forward.

You have learned that Michael's protection is not only a barrier against what is external, but an inner light that awakens within you the courage and confidence to face any challenge. Yes, he protects you, but he also strengthens you, revealing that true security is a state of being, a peace that grows within, as you allow yourself to trust, surrender, and open to his light.

Throughout this journey, you have experienced the transformative power of Michael's shield and sword, and now carry within you a new understanding of protection and purpose. These sacred symbols are not merely metaphors, but spiritual realities that help you access your own potential. Each time you invoke his presence, you remind yourself of the ability to cut through the bonds of the past, to dissolve shadows with the power of blue light, and to establish boundaries that shield and empower you.

This book has invited you to open your heart to receive, while also reminding you of the importance of giving, of balancing the forces of action and rest, and of finding a state of harmony that resonates within and around you. By internalizing these teachings, you begin to walk with greater lightness, knowing that Michael's strength is present in each step, in every choice, in every word.

Michael, the warrior of light, the guardian, remains by your side. He accompanies you in moments of decision, offers clarity when doubt arises, and inspires courage when fear threatens. He is the beacon that guides the way, but he is also the mirror that reflects your own light and wisdom. As you cultivate this connection, you will find that signs of his presence become clearer, that your intuition grows stronger, and that your sense of safety increases with each new day.

The conclusion of this reading is not an end, but an invitation to continue the journey. The connection with Michael is a continuous building, a relationship that strengthens as you allow yourself to trust, to open up, and to evolve. He will always be by your side, in every situation where you need protection, strength, or peace. And by keeping this connection alive, you not only find security but discover the true freedom to be who you are, to express the truth that resides in your heart.

May you continue to walk with the strength and peace of Archangel Michael, recognizing that his light is always guiding you. The true power of Michael manifests in your life not only as protection but as a call for you to live authentically, courageously, and fully. The journey continues, and with Michael at your side, each step reveals new horizons and a peace that nothing can shake.

www.ingramcontent.com/pod-product-compliance
Lightning Source LLC
LaVergne TN
LVHW040050080526
838202LV00045B/3558